WAR'S
FORGOTTEN
WOMEN

WAR'S FORGOTTEN WOMEN

British Widows of the Second World War

MAUREEN SHAW & HELEN D. MILLGATE

First published 2011

The History Press
The Mill, Brimscombe Port
Stroud, Gloucestershire, GL5 2QG
www.thehistorypress.co.uk

British Library Cataloguing in Publication Data.
A catalogue record for this book is available from the British Library.

ISBN 978 0 7524 6179 3

Typesetting and origination by The History Press
Printed in Great Britain
Manufacturing managed by Jellyfish Print Solutions Ltd

CONTENTS

ACKNOWLEDGEMENTS

We are greatly indebted to the following who answered our request for information:

Anne Anslow, Mrs Barbara Arnold, Michael B. Bishop, Chris Beatty, Mrs E. Ball, Catharine Barnett, David Blackburn, Phyliss Bliss, Bill Bombroff, Mrs Jane Burge, Sheila Cameron, Mrs M.H. Capon, Mrs Vera Capon, Clive Carter, M.R. Coleman, Mrs Mary Cook, Mrs O.L. Cooke, Kay Davey, Ann Doward, Pauline Dumbrill, Mrs A. Eastland, David Emery, Bob Grainger, Mrs Daphne Hackling, Mrs Hilary Hare, Rosemary Hockney, Margaret Hothi, Mrs S. Hennessy, Mrs Joyce Hickling, Barry Ison, Mrs Betty Jennings, Peter J. Jewell, Roma Ogilvie-Watson, P. O'Keefe, Barbara Lane, Sally Lawson, Ann Linford, Mrs N. Lestrange, Miss Mawson, Mrs E.M. Martin, Mary Monk, Ann Muller, Colin Newman, James Paice MP, Wilf Pearson, Vivienne Parslow, Roy Pickard, Mrs D.M. Pullen, Maureen Renfrew, Mrs M. Richardson, Reina Richardson, Mrs Elizabeth Roberts, Kathleen Shore, Helen Smith, Mrs Josephine Smith, Mrs M. Sonday, Michaela Spooner, Mrs Janet Stubbins, Elizabeth Tebbs, Bill Thompson, Foster Watson, Valerie Watson, Mrs R. West, Mrs B. Willis, Irene Willis, Pauline Williams, Bill Wilkinson, Carol Woodward, Mrs Olive Worton.

We are also especially grateful to Debbie Roberts at the Thompson Library, Staffordshire University, for access to the Iris Strange Collection and to Dr Janis Lomas who has allowed us the use of her work on war widows. Thanks also to Gordon Graham for the KET article based on Jim Gibson's account, David Blackburn for his poem and David Woodcock for his generosity with the GAFLAC material. It has been a great pleasure to make the acquaintance of Elizabeth (Betty) Tebbs whose life story has been quite inspirational. Gillian Farrar and Peter Francis shared their knowledge of the Royal British Legion and Ted Holmes was able to clarify the Australian pension structure. Gillian Grigg MBE, chairman of the War Widows' Association from 2008–11 has been most helpful. Finally we must thank our husbands for their patience and understanding while we worked on this project. They have given us their total support and encouragement at all times.

CHRONOLOGY

1939–45 .... The Second World War. The war widows' pension is regarded as unearned income and taxed at the highest rate.

1946 .... Jessie Vasey, widow of General George Vasey, establishes a war widows' guild in Melbourne, Victoria.

1948 .... War Widows' Guild of Australia founded.

1971 .... Laura Connolly's case is published in the *Sunday Express*. She calls on all British war widows to band together.

1972 .... Jill Gee constitutes the War Widows' Association (WWA) and is elected its first chairman. The initial aim was to have the war widows' pension declared non-taxable income. The WWA presents their first petition to 10 Downing Street and Mrs Gee unofficially lays a small wreath at the Cenotaph on behalf of the WWA.

1970s .... Mrs Iris Strange joins the WWA and becomes Secretary.

1975 .... First official War Widows' service at the Cenotaph, the day before the national Remembrance Day service.

Armed Forces Pension Scheme introduced. All service personnel serving for more than two years were henceforth entitled to a pension. The widows of those who have died either in service or in retirement where death is attributable to time in the service will receive a Forces Family Pension in addition to the War Widows' Pension.

1976 .... Removal of 50 per cent of the tax on
                         war widows' pensions.

1977 .... Jill Gee resigns as chairman of the WWA.

1979 .... The remaining 50 per cent tax is
                         removed, and war widows' pensions
                         become entirely free from tax. WWA
                         begin fight for parity of pensions for all
                         war widows.

1982 .... The Falklands Conflict.

                         Representatives from the WWA invited
                         to take part in the official muster
                         and march past the Cenotaph on
                         Remembrance Sunday.

                         Iris Strange forms the breakaway British
                         War Widows and Associates (BWWA).

1986 .... For the first time a plot is reserved for
                         the WWA at the Field of Remembrance
                         at Westminster Abbey.

1989 .... The first ever parade of war widows at
                         the Remembrance Service at the Royal
                         Albert Hall.

                         Nicholas Winterton MP spearheads the
                         cross-party campaign for parity for all
                         war widows in the House of Commons.

1990 .... The government finally agrees to pay all
                         pre-1973 war widows an MOD supple-
                         mentary pension of £40 weekly tax-free
                         to compensate for the lack of a Forces
                         Family Pension.

1991 .... The WWA becomes a registered charity.

INTRODUCTION

THE RECENT activities of the British armed forces in Iraq and Afghanistan have currently stimulated an interest in the circumstances of the widows of men who die on active service. But what has happened to the women left bereft after the 1939–45 war? Some of them are still alive; certainly many of their children are. What kind of a life have they had since the untimely death of their husbands and fathers? Maureen Shaw was herself the only child of a soldier who died on active service in Burma and who vividly recalls her own childhood, with no father figure, no siblings and always short of money. She pondered the subject for many years then one day asked me if I would be interested in enquiring into the matter with her since I had previously published works on the war period. Together we decided to trawl the library catalogues to see what turned up; nothing did, though there may have been a few references tucked away that we missed. Look in the index of any of the myriad histories of both world wars and the word 'widow' almost never appears. However what did turn up was a plethora of publications concerning the women widowed by the American Civil War, the Indian Mutiny, colonial strife and even a few about the First World War, but nothing at all of the Second. There are indeed the occasional references, in books on single-parent families, social service reports, and in the minutes of charitable organisations, but no more.

We hope to fill the gap. There has been an excellent response to our request for information, which appeared in many regional newspapers, and some of the replies are heartbreaking. The one quoted below from Mrs B. Willis of Plymouth was reason enough for us to persevere:

My Father died on the Russian Convoys (7.1.1943) and my mother was left with three young children, aged 10 years (me) 8 years (brother) and sister 5 years. My Father died of his wounds and had a naval burial in Murmansk, Russia, so we have never been able to visit a grave. Mum also lost a baby son ten months before we lost Dad. As regards to the financial straits we were left in, Yes, we became poor, as for the first week after losing my father as he died on a Friday and didn't live a full 'pay week' my mother received just 19 shillings. My father when he died was an Acting Petty Officer (aged 32) and my mother's pension became £2.12/- a week to keep four of us. I do not know what her Naval Allowance was before that but I do know that our lives did change and Mum used to feel very bitter about the things we had to do without (basic things we needed, not luxuries). She sold our cheese and sweet [ration] and part of our clothing coupons to neighbours for money to buy coal and pay the gas and electric bills, we had no radio until a kind neighbour lent us an old one. To this day I can't eat cheese...

There is so much more I could say; Mum died in December 2002, just three weeks before the 60th anniversary of losing my father and she never, ever forgot the struggle and the feeling of abandonment she got when she needed help for herself and her children. When Mum became frail she was given a small sheltered accommodation, a bunga-low, eighteen months before she died. I rang the Naval Association for help with removal costs of £100. I was told it was our responsibility to pay for it, even though we are now pensioners. So you see why Mum never got over the feeling of being of no importance.

I do hope this missive will be of some help to you with your research as being a War Orphan I am glad that at last someone is showing an

interest in our lives and the sadness we had to bear without any support from any outside authority. Thank you for your interest.

That many war widows 'never got over the feeling of being of no
importance' is reiterated by Janis Lomas in her brief to a 2010
conference on Women, War and Remembrance:

> The anguish and loss they felt was exacerbated by the neglect and
> indifference they felt surrounded them. Their pension provision was
> minimal and subject to income tax. Remembrance for them was per-
> sonal not collective as they were excluded from Remembrance Day
> ceremonies and had little opportunity for their grief and loss to be
> acknowledged within the public arena.

Before we examine the hardships undoubtedly suffered by the
widows of servicemen, and indeed all widows, we must take into
account the entire wartime scenario and the decade of austerity
which followed for it wasn't until the mid-1950s that normality –
if there ever is such a thing – returned. Rationing for example did
not entirely disappear until 1954 and the winter of 1946–47 was
truly appalling. A dire shortage of coal (the sole source of heating
in most homes) exacerbated the sheer misery of that winter. For
years after the war ended there was a critical shortage of building
materials, therefore housing, and everything necessary to make
life comfortable, such as transport, clothing, household furnish-
ings etc. were also in short supply. It took months, even years,
to convert factories back from arms production to their former
usage. Particularly during the war every woman running a household was constrained by rationing and shortages of unrationed
goods which usually entailed queuing for just about everything.
She had to 'make do and mend' as was constantly exhorted by
the Ministry of Information posters, turning old garments into
schoolboy shorts, re-knitting used wool for jumpers and turning
old curtains into dresses. With all scrap metal going to the war
effort it became almost impossible to buy a saucepan or a kettle.
Every day presented a challenge and the majority of working-class

families lived from week to week; there was no fallback. The stigma of the Poor Law remained, as Eleanor Rathbone writes in the 1920s: 'It has made the "stigma of pauperism" a very real thing; so real that many widows, the best of their kind, those in whom the tradition of self-help is strongest and who are more sensitive to slights, are indeed "deterred" from seeking the help so grudgingly offered.' The stigma and horror of degradation for resorting to the Poor Law for assistance was still very much in evidence until the National Insurance Act came into force. People would almost rather starve than beg for handouts.

At the beginning of the Second World War, one of the Mass Observation diarists, a door-to-door salesman, agonises because he must borrow £5 in order to make ends meet and then can only pay it back in £1 installments over a period of months. Still living in the family home at the age of twenty-eight, he writes that they can only afford two meals daily, breakfast and high tea. He complains that prices are constantly rising while his total income for a family of three adults remains at an average £2 10s. This level of poverty was not unique: anyone not from the wealthier classes who lived through the period can remember the day-to-day struggle to make ends meet.

The Blitz exacerbated the already chronic housing shortage (even by 1951 it was estimated that there was a shortfall of 1.5 million houses). Apart from the more obvious problems raised by re-housing the victims of bombing and putting up with evacuees, there was the constant movement of servicemen and their families, war workers et al. The some 12,000 people working at Bletchley Park for example all had to be billeted in the surrounding area. Servicemen's wives frequently moved in with relatives, particularly when their husbands were sent overseas. It was cheaper and perhaps offered some back-up and emotional support but it could also make life harder. One case quoted in a BBC programme was that of a young mother of three who moved back into her parents' home when her husband went overseas. She and the three small children occupied a single room shared with a widowed sister and her child. Quite often the wife then took the opportunity to do war work, make money and get out of the house. Most people lived in rented accommodation, and a lower income often meant eviction.

It should also be remembered that following the French surrender in June 1940 there was a very real fear of invasion, though probably few civilians were truly aware of the United Kingdom's extreme vulnerability at that time. It was not until the middle of 1943 that they could breathe a collective sigh of relief. Vast numbers of women were to spend these and subsequent months or years without the support (physical, emotional and sexual) of their husbands. Many wives perforce had to take on the role of head of the family, and they became used to making the decisions. In the worst cases – if they became prisoners of war for example – a man could be away for five years. (*When Daddy Came Home* by Barry Turner and Tony Rennell illustrates much of this.) One of our correspondents Elizabeth Tebbs, a soldier's wife with one child, says that when her husband was killed there was no noticeable immediate difference in her life because she had not seen him for a year.

All this must be taken into consideration when examining the situation of war widows during the war itself. Post-war, the introduction of the National Health and Insurance Service which came into force on 5 July 1948 at least relieved the low income groups from the burden of medical fees – sometimes 7s 6d for a doctor's housecall – and introduced a minimum widow's pension. The earnings rule was dropped in the 1960s but widows' pensions were not deemed to be tax-free until 1979. After 1979 widows were certainly better off financially, and were even more so from 1989 when, after an intensive campaign by the War Widows' Association (WWA) supported by the press and in Parliament, the widows from the Second World War were given parity with those widowed after 1973.

For most women no financial benefit could compensate for the loss of a husband. In a war when men die young it is even more tragic. What is surprising is the proportion of young widows in our small survey who never considered remarriage. Perhaps no other man could live up to the memory of the lost love, and so these women were, for the rest of their (often long) lives, bereft.

Using various sources – including Hansard (the record of parliamentary debates), BBC archives, the Iris Strange Collection held at Staffordshire University, the records of charitable organisations etc – but principally the personal experiences of the widows and children left behind after the havoc of the Second World War, we have hopefully gathered sufficient material to speak for them.

One

PENSIONS –
THE EARLY YEARS

MOST DEVELOPED countries in the world today have some form of state pension for the sick, aged and widowed. For war widows the system everywhere is far more complicated, a 'minefield' according to one official who has made a particular study of the subject. Another official described it succinctly as a 'headbanger'. In our investigation of the procedure in this country we have grappled with war widows' pensions, war disablement pensions, the Armed Forces Pension Scheme, the Armed Forces Compensation Scheme and the Veterans' Agency. We have looked at the workings of the inter-service charitable organisations and the labyrinthine National Assistance and Housing Benefit programmes to name but a few. The War Widow's Pension was intended to support her in compensation for the untimely death of her husband in the service of his country. Simply that. In 1988 an elderly war widow interviewed by the *Liverpool Post* said: 'I never had the chance to bear my husband's children. We were only married for two years and he was away a lot of that time anyway.' She described her War Widow's Pension as being an award for her loss and her husband's sacrifice: 'It is compensation for something very special and is not like any other form of income.'

All governments of course have a duty to the wider electorate not to favour one group above another. They must investigate the facts and review their resources. Sometimes even the best-laid schemes have unforeseen consequences. Edward Conway, economics editor of the *Daily Telegraph*, cited the case of one Getrude Janeway to illustrate the point that no government should make a promise that it could not afford to keep. In 2003 Mrs Janeway died at the age of ninety-three. She had spent her last few years bedridden, deploring the activities of the young and intoning the odd prayer or two. There was nothing particularly unusual about that, except that Mrs Janeway was the very last of the American Civil War widows, widows of a war that ended in 1865. Looking at the dates, this would seem to be impossible but Gertrude appears to have been both shrewd and far seeing. At the age of eighteen she had escaped poverty by marrying a Civil War veteran of eighty-one who had joined up in 1864 when he himself was eighteen years old. When she died, Getrude was in receipt of an annual pension of $420 relating to a war fought 140 years earlier. This was something of an aberration and one not foreseen by the politicians of the day who had devised the pension scheme. It is a salutary tale and an anomaly even in the often more generous American pensions structure.

On a lighter note, illustrating the undoubted fact that there were some scheming women around, Alistair Cooke in his book *American Journey* relates the tale of skulduggery at the vast USAAF base at San Antonio in Texas during the Second World War. There was apparently a group of 'determined' young ladies who made a career and a good living by marrying newly fledged Air Force officers just before they were posted overseas: 'Once the recent husband has gone to glory they register under another name, receive another Post Office box number and proceed to seek another mate' also destined to be shortly sent into a war zone and whose future was 'promisingly hazardous'.

At the end of the American War of Independence in 1781 the fledging government of that new state undertook to pay a pension of a half salary to officers' widows for a period of seven years. This was extremely generous for a country whose very existence was still shaky. Nevertheless it set a precedent for a generous pension scheme for the widows of American servicemen, which still exists today. During the 1992 Iraq War it was noted that the pensions for British war widows compared very unfavourably with the American equivalent. In the USA Dependency and Indemnity (DIC) has been paid in some form or other to survivors of servicemen since the 1774–78 American War of Independence (or the Revolutionary War as it is known in the USA). After the First World War the system was changed to a form of life insurance, which did away with the discrepancies between officers and other ranks, and this was the system in place during the Second World War. In 1951 Congress replaced this with a new scheme by which servicemen were not required to pay any premiums but the government would provide monthly payments to the surviving spouse and any children tax-free. A proviso was that widows would lose their pensions if they remarried. In 2003 a further amendment stated that a surviving spouse of fifty-seven years or older would be allowed to remarry and retain DIC benefits. One wonders why fifty-seven?

In Britain the official process took much longer. By 1708 British governments were paying pensions to the widows of officers killed in action but army and navy support for the common soldier's widow was practically non-existent. In her article 'Delicate Duties' Janis Lomas gives a comprehensive account of the evolution of financial support for war widows from charity handout to fully state-funded pension. She emphasises the extent to which issues and morality played a large part. During the nineteenth century only single men were allowed to enlist in the British Army and a soldier required his commanding officer's permission if he wished to marry, a rule which was in place until well into the twentieth century. If permission was granted, his wife was henceforth regarded as being 'on-the-strength' of the regiment and eligible for such meagre benefits as the regiment might provide. A mere 4–6 per cent of the rank and file were actually allowed to marry, a percentage that the hierarchy thought sufficient to supply the number of women required to wash, sew and mend for the regiment. The wife of a soldier who married without official permission was regarded as being 'off-the-strength'. Thus officially she did not exist, was not entitled to any category of welfare and would not, should her husband die, be recognised as an army widow. The Admiralty went even further, refusing to acknowledge the existence of the wife of any sailor below the rank of admiral. As one naval officer declared: 'In the Navy they knew of no such appendage or encumbrance as a sailor's wife.'

Before the Crimean War, which began in 1854, the only source of help for off-the-strength war widows was the much-loathed Poor Law. But such were the stringent conditions imposed by the Poor Law administrators – for example that the children be taken into the workhouse – that many women preferred to resort to prostitution or work at menial jobs for starvation wages. The Crimean War proved to be the catalyst. For the first time the public was fully informed of the progress of a war by newspaper reporters, the electric telegraph and official correspondents and much publicity was given to the plight of war widows and their orphaned children and the lack of provision for them. A Patriotic Fund was established with voluntary contributions and a token sum from the War Office. This combination of voluntary effort plus official backing was thought to be the best solution to the problem for many years, even with the advent of state-funded pensions and allowances from December 1916.

The Patriotic Fund raised the considerable sum of £1.5 million. Fund administrators were to be accused of excessive frugality, giving only 4s a week to the widows of the lower ranks and even then with the proviso that the widow should be 'deserving of help'. The Royal Commissioners of the fund refused assistance to any widow who 'by profligate behaviour dishonours the memory of her husband or if, when capable of service, she remains idle and will not go into service'. The names of those who did receive help were published with the Patriotic Fund's Annual Report as parliamentary papers.

In the decades that followed the Crimean War, the War Office was still denying any responsibility for off-the-strength widows and orphans and the Poor Law Board was doing its best to reduce the number of claimants. Public concern for these widows and their children eventually led to the founding in 1885 of the

Soldiers' and Sailors' Families Association (SSFA) which, unlike the Patriotic Fund, assisted the off-the-strength wives and widows as well as those officially recognised. Again both bodies were in agreement that only those judged worthy of help were to receive it. The Victorians believed firmly in Samuel Smiles' philosophy of hard work, frugality, self-denial and thrift. It was therefore the lack of these virtues that caused poverty and hardship among the lower classes.

They say that war is the engine of change, and this time it was the Boer War (1899–1902) which was eventually to trigger the next step: state pensions for the widows of other ranks. During the Boer War, the Patriotic Fund and SSFA increasingly worked together and with the other charities that sprang up at the time in support of the troops in South Africa. Newspapers, both national and provincial, were prominent in raising funds but way out in front was the *Daily Mail*, first published in 1897 by Alfred Harmsworth (later Lord Northcliffe) and the first newspaper in Britain to target the wider public. It ran an eye-catching banner headline, sport and human interest stories and even had a women's section. Harmsworth promoted his newspaper's War Fund campaign by the inclusion of hugely sentimental and patriotic features but, above all, by commissioning a poem from one of the most famous poets of the day – Rudyard Kipling. All the proceeds from this poem were to be paid into a fund for soldiers and their dependants. On 16 October 1899 Kipling duly obliged with 'The Absent-Minded Beggar', which proved an instant success in Britain and indeed all around the world. Sir Arthur Sullivan set the poem to music that Kipling described as 'guaranteed to pull teeth out of barrel organs' and within weeks the country was obsessed with it. One can see from the following extract why it had the desired effect:

> That, while he saved the Empire, his employer saved his place
>> And his mates, that's you and me, looked out for her.
> He's an absent-minded beggar and he may forget it all,
>> But we do not want his kiddies to remind him

That we sent them to the workhouse
While their daddy hammered Paul.

It was a constant item in the theatres and music halls. *The Times* reported on 30 November 1899 that: '… in order to help swell the funds now being raised for the widows and orphans of those taking part in the war in South Africa, Mrs Beerbohn Tree had consented nightly to recite Mr R. Kipling's poem "The Absent Minded Beggar". Mrs Tree's fee for doing so, £100 per week, the whole of this without deductions, she will hand over to the Fund.' Mrs Tree was probably England's best-known actress. Kipling became somewhat weary of the fervour aroused by his poem but at the same time proud of his ability to raise money to help the 'third class carriages' as he called the soldiery.

Kipling's poem did tend to eclipse the efforts of other charities. The *Daily Mail* went on to set up the Absent Minded Beggar Relief Corps which operated throughout the war aiding servicemen's families along with other charities. The activities and reporting of the corps' charitable works helped give maximum publicity to the war in South Africa.

By such measures the conscience of the nation was aroused and public clamour increased in favour of state pensions for the widows of non-commissioned officers (NCOs) and other ranks. Lord Salisbury's Conservative government bowed to public pressure and pensions for the widows of soldiers of other ranks were subsequently introduced in 1901, with certain provisos. Only widows who were on-the-strength would receive a weekly pension of 5s per week plus 1s 6d for each child. Off-the-strength widows would receive nothing at all, nor would the widows of black soldiers, though 'discretionary' payments might be made. The pension would be forfeit should a widow remarry or commit misconduct. One such case in the National Archives is of a widow granted the 5s pension in 1901 only to have it withdrawn in 1902 on the birth of an illegitimate child. It was not restored until twenty years later. Another case quoted was that of a Mrs Josephine Downey who had been left a widow with two small children when

her husband, Pte James Downey of the 2nd Battalion Royal Lancs.,
was killed in South Africa in August 1900. In June 1901 she wrote
to the War Office enquiring whether she was entitled to a pension
under the new regulations. The application was turned down on
the grounds that Pte Downey had not been killed in action, or died
of wounds, but had instead died in a tram accident at Paardekop.
Although the regulations were subsequently amended to include
such situations, in practice it was never to be easy for widows to
obtain a pension in those circumstances.

The First World War was the catalyst for further reforms. In the
very first week of the war in August 1914 the Asquith government
announced pensions for both off-the-strength widows and the
widows of volunteers. The will was there, but the way was not,
and the administrative machinery in place struggled to cope with
a huge increase in pension applications. It was chaotic and by
now the 5s pension was totally inadequate, often late and in many
cases, totally absent. Many war widows were forced to apply to
the Patriotic Fund, which relied on the SSFA to validate the claims,
and even then it was the National Relief Fund that actually handed
out the cash. The time that it took to go through this procedure
did not help the already grieving widow. Janis Lomas points out
that even when the pension was paid, it had to be supplemented
by the Patriotic Fund to the tune of 7s or 9s weekly, according to
the age of the supplicant and her 'station in life'. The War Office,
even in those first few months, was totally swamped by the rising
death toll and had to use the SSFA as its agent of administration.
The fate of war widows and their children was therefore dependent on the judgement of a band of volunteers.

Disquiet in Parliament and increasing public protest regarding the suitability of a charitable organisation for this purpose
led in 1915 to the setting up of a select committee to investigate
the pensions procedure. It concluded that control should be
removed from the charities and handed back to the state. They
also proposed to double the minimum War Widow's Pension
to 10s a week plus 5s for the first child, 3s 6d for the second
and 2s for any subsequent offspring. Although the committee's

recommendation was for state administration of pensions the task was rather bizarrely given to the newly constituted Statutory Committee of the Royal Patriotic Fund (RPF). This committee was to frame the regulations, decide the amount of individual pensions and, if called for, hand out supplementary charitable payments. Janis Lomas describes these supplementary payments as being 'designed to preserve the class position and income of the recruit from higher up the social scale'. In addition the Statutory Committee was given the power to decide whether a woman was 'worthy' of a pension. If there were doubts 'administration in trust' was invoked; in effect her pension was allotted only as the trustees saw fit. In lieu of a cash payment she might be given food tickets or have her rent paid and there would be regular reports regarding her behaviour by a committee member and by the police. Only when these reports were consistently favourable was she allowed to handle her own money. The committee also had the power to withdraw the pension completely. This patronising attitude, an echo of the Poor Law, was now set in government legislation as a means of social control.

Needless to say the Statutory Committee was exceedingly unpopular with the general public who viewed it as yet another abdication of responsibility by the government. Many organisations, including the trades unions, the Independent Labour Party and Sylvia Pankhurst's National League of Rights for Soldiers' and Sailors' Wives and Relatives among others, clamoured for fully state-funded pensions, free from any sniff of a charity handout. The government, reeling from the increasing number of deaths at the front, bowed to public pressure and created the Ministry of Pensions to be responsible for decisions regarding pensions and allowances. The Statutory Committee was quietly disbanded but its function of administering monies 'in trust' was transferred to yet another committee, this time within the Ministry of Pensions. It was the state that now decided the 'worthiness' of a widow. The state demanded that the war widow acknowledge her husband's sacrifice by her own irreproachable behaviour in order to be worthy of a pension. This Special Grants Committee also had the authority to remove children from their mother and place them under the aegis of the Ministry of Pensions if it was suspected that the children were 'suffering from neglect or proper care'. Even if convicted of no offence, a widow might be judged unfit on moral grounds and her children taken away. She had no right of appeal, a phenomenon that still exists in the twenty-first century.

Unlike the War Office, which refused to pursue anonymous tip-offs, the Special Grants Committee investigated every hint, written or verbal, that they received regarding possible immoral behaviour. The committee enforced the Ministry's rulings to the point of harshness as is illustrated by one incidence when it not only revoked the widow's pension but also barred her from claiming Parish Relief, thus leaving her destitute. There were 1,200 local War Pensions Committees by the end of the war, often formed from existing committees of the RPF and SSFA. They all seem to have been obsessed by the perception of 'misconduct' and widows were particularly vulnerable to any malicious gossip. Even if the rumour or accusation was unfounded, the investigation, committee visits and police reports must have been a nightmare for any woman.

In 1919, after the end of the war, yet another select committee was set up to review the entire pension arrangements. It recommended a minimum weekly sum of 26s for war widows plus children's allowances. A childless widow under the age of forty was to be awarded the princely sum of £1 a week (unbelievably this remained in place until the 1960s). The widow of a 2nd lieutenant would receive £120 per annum, others more, commensurate with their late husband's rank. (In 1916 Capt. Robert Hopewell's widow was awarded £100 per annum. Eleanor Allum, wife of Pte Allum, got 13s 9d weekly). Yet despite these increases in pensions the granting of a pension was not automatic and a war widow still had to prove her entitlement. Even if their 'worthiness' was not in dispute there were many other reasons for refusing a pension. Pensions could be and were refused on often flimsy grounds. Many widows of men who died from a disease or injury while on active service were refused a pension if 'the man's death from either disease or injury was due, or partly due, to his own negligence'. This ruling remained in force until 1943. Other women were affected by the Seven Year Rule, which stated that a widow was only entitled to a pension if her husband had died of wounds, injuries or disease 'within seven years of his removal from duty on account of such disease'. This harsh ruling meant that wives who had devotedly nursed their husbands for years could, in theory, be left destitute simply by keeping their husbands alive too long. One ex-serviceman wrote to his MP James Hogge in February 1919:

> I am in a dilemma. It is now three years since I contracted this disease and, unless I die within four years from now, my wife and children will be deprived of their pension. I know that by taking the greatest possible care of my life I might live a few years longer, but what a horrible feeling it is to me to think that if I prolong my life by care beyond that time limit, by doing so I leave my wife and children destitute.

The carnage of the First World War resulted in large numbers of war widows, immediately recognisable in their black 'widow's weeds'. One in eight would themselves die within a year of losing a husband. The treatment of these very numerous war widows was, to say the least, insensitive, when for example, at the Victory celebrations, widows were only allocated seats after Queen Mary personally intervened hoping that 'the poor women will not be forgotten'. Original plans for Armistice Day observance after 1918 actually contained a proposal to exclude war widows. Thanks to a press campaign that led to questions being asked in Parliament, this proposal was dropped. Compare this to the attitude of the French government. When the chosen corpse for the *Poilu Inconnu*, France's Unknown Soldier, was being brought from Verdun to Paris, five war widows were given the honour of accompanying it.

The vast majority of war widows' pensions were never above subsistence level and were further eroded by the inflation of the

1920s. While Britain did not experience the massive inflation that happened in Germany, prices did rise faster than incomes and it was a constant struggle for the widow to feed and clothe her family. The Battlefield Tours offered by the travel agent, Thomas Cook & Sons after the First World War and much in vogue were quite beyond the reach of most war widows, even the economy version at around £10, let alone the luxury version at 35 guineas.

In the majority of cases the widow of a soldier killed in action faced few difficulties when applying for a pension, however, the widow whose husband had died after the end of the war of war injuries was far less fortunate. It was she who had to stand in front of a tribunal and prove that her husband's death was due to his war service. Reading through the various accounts by First World War widows of their struggles for a pension it is difficult to understand how the war pensions tribunals could be so intransigent. It would seem that any query – however slight – was excuse enough to refuse a pension. One situation that often arose concerned the widows of men married after their discharge from the army who subsequently died as a result of war injuries. Despite it being accepted that these men died of injuries received in the war their widows were refused a pension simply on the grounds that the marriage took place after discharge from the army. The authorities seemed to fear that a woman might marry in the hope of eventually getting a War Widow's Pension.

At Staffordshire University there is a valuable archive of letters from war widows of the First and Second World Wars known as the Iris Strange Collection. Iris was herself a war widow whose husband died while a prisoner of the Japanese during the Second World War and she was to become one of the women who fought for a fairer deal for widows like herself. There are many harrowing tales in the archive.

One First World War widow wrote that it had taken forty years for her to get her army widow's pension and even then it was backdated a mere two years. By the time her National Assistance payments were deducted she received the princely sum of £428, part of which she used to erect a headstone on her husband's grave. But even marriage to a serving soldier who later died as a result of his war service did not guarantee his widow a pension, as is illustrated by the following extract from the archive. Another woman wrote of her husband, a sergeant major in the Scots Guards and badly wounded in the First World War, who had decided to stay on in the army until he had completed twenty-one years' service after which he would be eligible for a pension. He died after almost twenty years' service as a result of his earlier war wounds but his wife was denied a War Widow's Pension on the grounds that they did not marry until 1922. This was despite living in barracks and her son having been born in a military hospital. Her husband was given a military funeral, complete with headstone inscribed 'In Honoured Memory' while she and her one-year-old baby were evicted from their home with a grand income of 15s weekly: 10s for the mother and 5s for the child.

For some women, remarrying was an option and hopefully an escape from grinding poverty. Janis Lomas quotes an MP who was reported as saying:

> The best thing that can happen to war widows is that they should get married again and their best chance of doing that is going out into the world [to work] and meet men – they are more likely to do that than by sitting at home waiting for the milkman.

In other words, get married again at the earliest opportunity and save the country some money! However for most women all that was available was hard, exhausting menial labour, generally without any security and always low paid, as is illustrated by many letters in the archive. These two are typical:

> I was left with 5 children. I took in knitting and sewing, I took in washing from the army camp – hard work. I worked in a house, washing, scrubbing and cleaning from 9–6...

> I had two boys so I used to take in washing for 9 families...

For these First World War widows the very last resort was Parish Relief, the remaining vestige of the Victorian Poor Law. In a country whose people have enjoyed the benefits of the Welfare State since 1948 it is difficult to understand how earlier generations dreaded 'going on the parish'. It was the final source of financial assistance open to the poorest of the poor but it was demeaning and humiliating, intentionally so, in order to deter the impoverished masses. One war widow with three sons, and another child expected, in receipt of a pension of £1 8s but after rent deduction left with 17s 6d to keep the whole family, was denied help because she was 'not destitute'. Another wrote that she and her three young children under four years of age had to live on the Poor Law for nine months: '… as you can imagine it was terrible.' A war widow's daughter born six weeks after her father died of his war injuries wrote to Iris Strange many years later:

> I remember her [her mother] telling me once how she swallowed her pride and asked for help from the Poor Fund and two shilling and sixpence was flung across the counter at her as if she were dirt. She never asked again.

Many women after nursing a war-wounded husband would spend their last penny on his funeral. At a time when working-class people saved all their lives for a decent funeral, a respectable burial was regarded as highly important. In the collection there is a very distressing letter from a First World War widow who, after nursing her husband, could only afford '… a pauper's burial with other people. He lies like a park, no surrounds, only No 9'. Obviously the War Widow's Pension – or indeed any widow's pension – was not intended to allow her to live in idle luxury. It was meant to cover only the most basic needs, so unless she was able to get outside work, and sometimes even then, she was condemned to a life of grinding poverty:

> I had 13/6d a week for myself and my child. After a year I got back to work and, after ups and downs, have got through scrubbing floors,

whitewashing cellars and ceilings, going out washing for two shillings and sixpence a day from 8 a.m. to 8 p.m.

Little it would seem changed in the 1920s and 1930s. Real wages barely increased during this period; they were years of industrial depression and the widow's pension reflected the general trend. The 1925 Widows' Act, which made provision for a weekly sum of 10s for the widow, 5s for the first child and 3s for subsequent children, was still causing bitterness in the 1940s. There are many references in Hansard to these '10/- Widows'. In her book *The Disinherited Family*, Eleanor Rathbone quotes the 1921 census, which lists the astonishing figure of 306,000 widows with 606,500 dependant children. Of that number 103,000[*] were service widows with 75,200 dependant children. Hardly surprising then that any government, whether Labour, Liberal or Conservative, baulked at the prospect of providing any widow with a decent and fair income.

---

[*]   Difficult to gain exact figures, Janis Lomas quotes the number of War Widows receiving a pension as 191,317; official estimates have 908,371 killed or died in the First World War (figure includes Empire troops).

Two

PENSIONS – THE YEARS OF STRUGGLE

IT **IS** now more than sixty-five years since the end of the Second World War and while the recollections of those involved may not always be totally accurate, there is no doubt that the vast majority of war widows after that conflict did for many years find the War Widow's Pension quite inadequate for their needs:

> I know in those days she [my mother] had a job to manage on the War Widow's Pension and there was no help to bring me up.

> My mother feels that people have no idea of the financial hardships and lack of support for Second World War widows.

> It was very difficult at first. Very little pension until late in life.

The widow would be informed of her husband's death by a telegram from the War Office. This would be followed by information regarding her entitlement to a pension, the amount of which varied according to the rank of the deceased. It was a two-tier system: the higher rate was paid when the widow was aged over forty, incapable of supporting herself due to ill-health or looking after a child or children, and the lower rate applied to those under forty years of age and childless. In 1940 the widow of a top-ranking officer such as a field marshal or equivalent would receive a pension of £600 per annum while a lieutenant's widow would

receive £90 per annum. Other ranks were divided into six clas-
sifications and, in 1940, the widows' pensions ranged from 30s a
week (higher rate) to 15s 6d a week (lower rate) for the widow of
a private. These rates were amended as the war continued and by
1946, the field marshal's widow was receiving £700 per annum,
the lieutenant's widow £150, the warrant officer's 40s a week and
the private's widow a mere 20s. Unlike all other war widows who
did get increases in their pensions over the years, albeit small, the
private's widow's pension remained – unbelievably – at 20s until
1967. Informing a woman of the death of her husband and her
pension entitlement was the extent of government involvement;
there were no helpful leaflets or information pamphlets for further guidance. She was now on her own and, above all, she had
no organisation to speak for her. It would be thirty years before
British war widows were able to speak with one voice.

During the Second World War Britain's well documented and
efficiently organised pension scheme was quite detailed in differ-
entiating between officers and other ranks and meticulous in the
classification of those other ranks. However it is difficult for any
system to be foolproof. Anomalies arose and so much depended
on the individual interpretation of rules and regulations: all that
was of little comfort to a widow who had so much to deal with at
a time when she was most vulnerable. One daughter wrote most
bitterly of her mother's situation. Her father joined the RAFVR
(Royal Air Force Volunteer Reserve) and was sent out to the Far
East. In 1942 he was reported 'missing, presumed killed'. He
actually died in April 1942 but his family did not know this until
the end of the war:

> My mother was told she could not have an allowance because he
> was 'presumed' killed, neither could she have a pension because he
> was posted 'missing'. She was means-tested and for most of the war
> received 27/6d a week.

When a serviceman is killed in action his wife's position is clear:
she is then technically a war widow and receives a War Widow's

Pension. This applies to all three services. The situation is less clear if the serviceman is reported missing as in the above example, which happens perhaps most frequently with naval personnel. Obviously when ships are at sea for long periods, and operating in wartime conditions, communications are not perfect, and the Admiralty was quite properly reluctant to declare a seaman dead until certain of the fact. Indeed many wives informed that their husbands were 'missing' were asked to keep the information to themselves and their immediate family who were similarly asked to keep the matter confidential. This was so that an incident of war 'should not find its way to the enemy'. The constant strain of worrying about her husband's fate must have been made unbearable by the need to keep quiet in the face of enquiries about him from friends and acquaintances.

Gladys Oxenham's husband was reported missing in June 1940; she was informed that for a period of eight weeks from notification the Allotment and Marriage Allowance would continue to be paid at the rate previously in force:

Marriage Allowance	23 shillings a week
Allotment	26 shillings a week

For the next nine weeks until the last payment in October the rate would be:

Marriage Allowance	23 shillings a week
Allotment	14 shillings a week

Mrs Oxenham's husband was declared dead on 20 October 1941, which leaves a gap of almost twelve months.

Winifred Emery received a telegram in June 1940 telling her that her husband Able Seaman Leonard Emery was missing and believed to be a prisoner of war. She received a further letter from the Admiralty dated 2 July 1940:

As your husband Leonard Emery (Able Seaman, Royal Fleet Reserve P/ SSX 12063) is not included in the list of survivors or in the list of those known to have been killed, My Lords Commissioner of the Admiralty must continue to regard him officially as 'missing' though they regret to have to state that in their opinion the possibility of his being still alive is extremely remote.

In January 1941 the Admiralty reported that no further information had come to light; meantime Winifred Emery had received a similar seventeen-week pay arrangement to Gladys Oxenham. Official letters from the Royal Navy advised recipients to contact the Royal Naval Benevolent Society if in need, therefore it seems reasonable to assume that both Mrs Oxenham and Mrs Emery received some kind of interim allowance when the seventeen weeks had elapsed.

When Ruby Coleman's husband Harry was reported missing in December 1940 she too received the usual notification of the eight- and nine-week payment of allowances; the last payment to be made on 24 April 1941. His death was actually confirmed in May 1941 and Mrs Coleman then received an application form for a pension. The accompanying letter informed her that the marriage allowance would be continued for a limited period but would be 'in the nature of an advance on account of any pension which you may be awarded and will be taken into consideration in the event of such award'. An extract from Admiralty Fleet Orders July/September 1941 states that, when a rating is missing:

Pay will continue to be credited to the Man's account for a period of 4 weeks from and including the date on which the casualty is notified to relatives, or until the date on which the fact or presumption of death is so notified, whichever is the earlier. Marriage allowance etc plus actual allotment will continue in issue during the period so covered; and for the next 13 weeks an Allowance will be issued on the basis [of death confirmed] unless in the meantime it is established that the rating is alive.

At the outbreak of the Second World War the Merchant Navy was solely a commercial fleet concerned with transporting goods from one country to another. The merchant seaman signed on for each voyage and was paid off when that voyage ended. In 1939 the government took steps to incorporate the Merchant Navy into the war effort, producing the T124X Agreement by which Merchant Navy personnel undertook to serve as a member of the Naval Auxiliary until the end of the war, in any vessel, or for any voyage to which the member was assigned. In 1942 a separate pension scheme was drawn up for the Mercantile Marines to deal with their particular circumstances. The aim was to provide compensation on a par with that of the Royal Navy (albeit with stricter entitlement conditions) to provide merchant seamen with compensation for the disabling effects of, or death due to, the added perils to which they were subjected because of the war or other conflicts. Pensions were awarded where the circumstances of war substantially increased the risk of the peril that caused the injury or death. The scheme did not cover injuries or death resulting from the normal risks of seafaring life – that is, those present in peacetime as well as in war. The pensions were paid at an equivalent naval rank.

The widow of a merchant seaman killed on war service was thus eligible for a War Widow's Pension. As in the Royal Navy, pay ceased at death and the widow received her allotment or 50s a week, whichever was the greater, for six weeks, then 50s for four weeks until the pension came through. If the officer or rating was reported missing:

> ...the wife will be paid as a widow is paid during the 10 weeks following the notification of the death. If the officer or rating continues to be 'missing' the wife will receive payment at the rate at which pension would be paid if she were a widow, provided that were she a widow, pension would actually be awarded.

Pity any widow who had to wade through the 'official speak' to comprehend what she could or could not have. By the 1940s some of the more severe rules surrounding entitlement to a War Widow's Pension had been changed. They were no longer obliged, as they had been in previous years, to produce their children or to have a

magistrate or similar figure of authority certify that their circumstances were unchanged; a system described by Elizabeth Eatherall,
one of five children whose father had died on the Somme, as
'degrading and designed to cause maximum inconvenience'. On
each occasion her mother had to prove that she still had five children and all had to be shown to the appropriate official.

If she remarried however, she must relinquish her pension, unless
she was the widow of an officer, in which case she could apply for
restoration if in need. A war widow was expected to lead a chaste
and respectable life, and if for example, she bore an illegitimate
child, her pension was stopped. Threats to report her for 'cohabita-
tion' so distressed one lady that she gave up her pension book. In
1961, according to Hansard's report of parliamentary proceedings
thirty-one widows had their pensions withdrawn because of cohab-
itation. In a disgraceful repetition of official attitudes after the First
World War, large numbers of women were refused a War Widow's
Pension on what would seem flimsy and spurious grounds.

When Francis Pople died in 1942 his widow fully expected to
automatically receive a War Widow's Pension. Her husband had
joined the Coldstream Guards in 1930, served for eight years in
the Far East and Palestine, then left the army but remained on
the Reserve List. Called back in 1939 he went to France with the
British Expeditionary Force (BEF) and was badly wounded at
Dunkirk where he had been forced to spend thirty-six hours in
the water. As a consequence he lost much of his hearing. He was
evacuated from Dunkirk to Shenley Military Hospital and then
sent home. After what seems to have been a somewhat perfunc-
tory medical examination he was returned to military duties. One
day, after posting a letter to his wife in which he said how much
worse his deafness had become due to a severe head cold, he was
knocked down and killed by a car. His wife was immediately
informed that as he had been killed off-duty there would be no
War Widow's Pension. The army paid Mrs Pople an allowance for a
limited period only: about three months. At her own expense Mrs
Pople had her husband's body brought home to Wells, Somerset
for burial. The cost of transporting his body was 14s, which was

deducted from the part week's pay that was due to her husband. Mrs Pople received the remaining 2s.

With no money coming in, the family had to move to a smaller house. They went from having all 'mod cons' to a house with no kitchen or bathroom and having to share an outside toilet with a neighbour. An outside tap supplied water. Mrs Pople was unable to work due to ill health, and indeed was advised not to as it might jeopardise her fight for a pension. The British Legion helped arrange charity from Parish funds. They also helped her to fight her case but it took nearly two years for the War Office to agree to pay Mrs Pople a War Widow's Pension and then only because: 'under revised rules your husband's death can be accepted as due to war service.'

As we have already mentioned, many women were to be refused a War Widow's Pension if their husbands died after the end of the war, despite their early deaths being attributable to war service. In the Iris Strange Collection there are many letters from women denied a pension after nursing a war-damaged husband. The government took the view that it was the widow's personal responsibility to prove that her husband had died because of his war service. Among the many moving letters in the archive is one from a woman whose husband came home a mental and physical wreck after three years of Japanese captivity during which he had slaved on the Burma railway. She then contracted tuberculosis from him, which resulted in them both being sent to a sanatorium and their son being fostered. They were later allowed home and her husband, still severely mentally disturbed, and imagining that he was still in a Japanese prison camp, tried to kill her. He was sent to a mental institution for six years. When he returned so did the tuberculosis and they were both ill for some time although by this time the 'wonder drug' streptomycin had become available. They were both pronounced cured but her husband had become deaf, due to a side effect of the drug. She had to work when and as she could because her husband had always been totally unfit for work. Eventually he died in his sleep. Despite such terrible suffering this woman was refused a War Widow's Pension. Why? Because he died in his sleep! She appealed against the decision, went before a Pensions Appeal Tribunal, and was again refused:

I went to the Tribunal and quite frankly if was a farce. I was in there about 5 minutes and was told 'Mrs D … what do you expect? The army was your husband's job and therefore you expect him to get killed or disabled, so how can you expect a war widow's pension.'

In the dossier assembled by the WWA in 1983 and sent to every MP, there is another very tragic case where the widow of a soldier who had received a high-disability pension was to be refused a War Widow's Pension:

The husband was terribly wounded at Dunkirk. He was sent back wrapped in a blanket with a note pinned to him which said 'Not to be disturbed – will not recover'. When the less injured had received attention this poor man was dealt with. He did survive but perhaps he would have preferred to have died. After two years he was sent home to his wife and young daughter with a permanent colostomy and his manhood gone forever, aged only twenty-six. He was 100% disabled and could not work. His wife cared for him and went out to work to keep the family. She nursed him through three nervous breakdowns and he died, aged fifty-two years, of a heart condition. His widow was crucified at the tribunal where it was implied that her husband had smoked himself to death. No one knew of the health hazard of smoking until long after the war and smoking had been this poor man's only pleasure. In fact it was encouraged for shock and nervous disorders. I know of no other country where a widow would have been denied her rightful pension in similar circumstances, but there are many here.

As late as 1986 the plight of ex-POWs held by the Japanese is still a subject of bitterness. C.W. Holtham, the chairman of Southend & District Far Eastern Prisoner of War Association writes:

The British Government insists that, once seven years has passed since discharge from active service it is for the individual to establish beyond 'reasonable doubt' [that] any illness can be linked with war-time privation or injury… Often it is only after death and post-mortem that

family fears are realised that the loved one has died as a direct or indi-
rect result of life in a Japanese Labour Camp. Then the widow has to
pursue an appeals claim for a pension through the DHSS [Department
of Health and Social Security]. That can take a year or even longer to
gain a hearing and, again, it is for her to prove... Delays in appeals
are frightful and many people are convinced they are simply being
'fobbed off'.

He goes on to compare the attitude of the British government
with that of the situation of ex-POWs in Canada where the veterans of the Far East campaign were automatically awarded a
sliding scale of generous disability pensions. All pensions, including widows' pensions, are increased annually at the rate of the
Consumer Price Index.

Another example in the Iris Strange Collection tells of a man
on a 100 per cent war disability pension who was discovered to
have been suffering from a rare form of cancer found only in the
Middle East where he spent much of his service. When he died
his widow was refused a pension on the grounds that his death
was not due to war service. When she appealed the tribunal disregarded his war disability pension and the cancer and reiterated
that his death was not due to his war service. Figures are unavail-
able for the number of women refused a War Widow's Pension
in the immediate post-war years but it is interesting to note that
even as recently as 1991 only 37 per cent of appeals were successful. It is shameful that women who had so devotedly nursed their
disabled husbands were denied a pension. They themselves were
effectively prevented from taking outside work and therefore prevented from building up some further pension provision for their
retirement. They faced a lonely and poverty-stricken old age and,
like their husbands, were casualties of war.

There were very few war widows who did not have to work
to supplement their pensions. As Janis Lomas points out, war
widows were expected to work and not be dependent on
the state. If a widow did work, her pension was added to her
earnings and she was taxed accordingly as a single person, as

explained later. Following the 1948 National Insurance Act, National Assistance was used to top up war widows' pensions in cases of extreme need, thus enabling governments to keep pensions at a low level. Those with small children were inevitably trapped into menial, low-paid, part-time jobs. In 1952 Hilda James was living in a basement in Fulham with her thirteen-year-old daughter and her eighty-three-year-old mother who was paralysed. As she could not leave her mother alone she took in dressmaking work. Her pension and rent allowance came to £3 weekly and she was given National Assistance of 5s 6d. When pensions went up by 7s the National Assistance was withdrawn. With a growing child she was effectively no better off; they could not even afford a radio.

Poverty and illness go hand in hand and both conditions are intensified by loneliness. The vulnerable war widow perforce had to deal with bureaucratic authorities, generally male dominated, on her own. As with the earlier widows of the First World War they, and their problems, tended to be swept under the carpet, disregarded and unrecognised yet any false step that brought them to the notice of these authorities could have serious consequences. It only took one malicious item of gossip or rumour reported to the powers that be for the pension to be withdrawn with dire effects for the widow and her children. Having a male friend was hardly a criminal offence, but the widow's right to a pension was subject to judgements by self-styled moralists; whoever heard of a man losing his pension because he had a female friend?

In her book *Stranger in the House* Julie Summers wonders why war widows in Britain took thirty years to organise themselves nationally, when in Australia the War Widows' Guild was formed immediately after the war. It is an interesting question. Perhaps after years of wartime conditions and rationing (which were to continue until 1954) women were exhausted and did not have the energy to organise effectively. Mavis Thorpe Clark in her book on the War Widows' Guild of Australia, *No Mean Destiny*, thinks it may be because all of the British people had been on the front line. Also, as previously mentioned, widows' names were not officially released. Even in 1979, despite requests from the WWA and individual MPs, the Department of Health and Social Security (DHSS) minister Reg Prentice still maintained that information held by the department should be kept in the strictest confidence and refused to release any names or addresses.

When the WWA was later asked why it had taken until the early 1970s to form an association they replied that attempts had been made, but without publicity they could not make contact. Newspapers did not generally publish their requests and they did not have sufficient funds to generate their own publicity. Once, when offered a slot on a nationwide programme on a Remembrance Sunday after the formation of the association, Iris Strange recalled:

> We eventually appeared for the final two and a half minutes of the programme which had included several minutes of Irish jollifications and other items which could have been shown at any time, while our impact date lasted only briefly after Remembrance Day. They asked why we had only recently formed our Association. I wrote and told the producer that the answer was in his own programme, we were always pushed to the bottom of the pile.

But perhaps the main reason was that the British did not have a Jessie Vasey. Jessie Mary Vasey was the widow of General George Vasey who had commanded the Australian forces in Greece and in New Guinea during the Second World War. In 1945, while on leave, he called to see the widow of one of his men who had been reported killed. He was appalled by her living conditions and resolved to help these young widows and their children when the war ended. As he set off to fly back to New Guinea he said to his wife: 'Look after the widows while I'm gone Jessie, and when I'm back I'll give you every atom of help I can.' Tragically, General Vasey was killed when his plane crashed near Cairns and Jessie Vasey herself, at the age of forty-five, became a war widow. Jessie honoured the promise that she made to her husband by founding the War Widows' Guild and never ceased to battle the authorities on behalf of its members.

The War Widows Association of Gt. Britain

The first meeting was held on January 8th. 1972 at 2 Burbo Mansions to form the War Widows Association of Gt. Britain.

Election of the Chairman, Mrs Jill Gee, was proposed by Mrs. Denise Lorimer. Seconded by Mrs. C. McColl.

Election of the Hon. Secretary, Mrs. Denise Lorimer, was proposed by Mrs. Jill Gee Seconded by Mrs. E. Morsman

Election of Hon. Treasurer, Mrs. Kathleen Woodside, was proposed by Mrs. Jill Gee Seconded by Mrs. N. Glover.

Election of Committee: Mrs. M. Dale
                         Mrs. C. Huggins
                         Mrs. E. McColl
                         Mrs. E. M. McMahon

It was agreed that re-election of officers and committee would be every two years.

A unanimous decision was taken to charge:-
                Entrance fee 25p
            Annual subscription fee 25p.
to cover the cost of stationery, typewriter, telephone, postage, travelling to present petitions and

for interviews with Members of Parliament.
Replying to every point put forward by any
Members of Parliament.

It was agreed the aims and objects of the
Association are:
        To defend the interests of the War
Widows and to help them in matters concerning
their welfare.
        Take steps with Official Organisations
on behalf of the War Widows.
        Give information about legislation
concerning War Widows.
        Inform the Government about the
situation of the War Widows and her children.

A decision was taken to hold a meeting
each month.

The next meeting will be held at 2 Burbo
Mansions on February 5th. 1972

Original minutes of first meeting of the War Widows' Association in January 1972.

WAR WIDOWS' PENSION RATES

Date	Amount per week	Date	Amount per week
1946 February	£1.15s.	1971 Sept.	£7.80
1952 May	£2. 2s.	1972 Oct.	£8.80
1955 Jan.	£2.12s. 6d.	1973 "	£10.10
1958 "	£3. 6s.	1974 July	£13.00
1961 April	£3.16s.	1975 April	£15.00
1963 May	£4.10s	1975 Nov.	£17.20
1965 April	£5. 5s.	1976 "	£19.80
1967 Nov.	£5.17s.	1977 "	£22.70
1969	£6.10s	1978 "	£25.30
		1979 "	£30.20
		1980 "	£35.30
		1981 "	£38.45
		1982 "	£42.70
		1983 "	£44.25
		1984 "	£46.55
		1985 "	£49.80
		1986 "	£50.30
		1987 April	£51.35
		1988 "	£53.50
		1989 "	£56.15

Please note how rarely we received rises before we formed our Pressure Group in 1971. At one point, from April 1961 to November 1969 the total increases we received amounted to only £2.14s.0d. and this was during the very affluent post war years when workers were receiving ever increasing wages such had never been known before.

Age Allowances:-

Age 65 years	£6.10
" 70 "	£12.20
" 80 "	£15.30

The above list of war widows' pension increases related only to war widows over the age of forty years. Those below that age received only 20/- a week, super taxed because it was claimed to be unearned income although it had been earned by our men's lives. A child's allowance was 7/- a week, untaxed, but did not even keep them in shoes. Most were in their early twenties when bereaved.

Please note the low rises since Conservatives came to office.

Today's service widows receive the above pension PLUS another pension from the MOD which is approximately £55.00 a week.

Table of war widows' pension rates.

Events took a different course in Britain as illustrated by these extracts from parliamentary debates recorded in Hansard. In April 1944 the government brought out a White Paper on service pay and allowances in which the minimum allowance for a serviceman's wife with children was increased to 35s a week with an allowance of 12s 6d for each child. The minimum war pension for a widow with children was increased to 32s a week with a flat rate allowance of 11s a week for each child. The question has to be asked: 'Why should a war widow's child have a lesser allowance? Did the government think a war widow's child ate less than other children?' On 5 May 1944 *The Times* Parliamentary Correspondent reported the members' criticism of this anomaly on the difference between the wife and the widow. Deputy Prime Minister Attlee rejected this criticism saying that:

> ...the matter had been carefully considered and the government were not prepared to equalize the position of wives and widows as, under certain circumstances, the Minister of Pensions had the power to supplement a war widow's pension by the amount to which her rent and

rates exceeded 8 shillings a week. The maximum rate of supplementa-
tion to be 12 shillings a week where rent and rates amounted to 20
shillings or more.

On the face of it this would seem fairly generous but other fac-
tors have to be taken into consideration. In 1938 a terraced house
could be had for 7s or 8s a week. Betty Tebbs was paying 11s 8d
but her house had what was then the luxury of indoor plumb-
ing and a garden. Taking into account the bombing and resultant
scarcity of accommodation it would be reasonable to assume
that renting a house in 1944 would cost appreciably more than
it had in 1941. Above all, the war widow, in contrast to the wife,
was taxed as a single woman and her income would be reduced
accordingly. Mrs Barbara Arnold would have been interested in
Mr Attlee's reply. When her husband was killed she was living
with her mother, having first gone to stay when she was expect-
ing a child. Her mother was a widow without a pension and Mrs
Arnold remembers that because they were living together neither
of them were entitled to housing benefits. Despite Mr Attlee's
premise, many MPs added their names to Sir Ian Fraser's motion
which asked the House of Commons to express the opinion that
neither a widow nor a child should be financially penalised by the
death or disablement of a husband or father on service and suggested that the government should reconsider the war pensions
proposals contained in the White Paper.

Questions about war widows' pensions were raised at regular
intervals by sympathetic MPs. In November 1944 Sir Smedley
Crooke asked the Chancellor if he was: '… aware of the injustice felt by war widows who have to pay tax on their widows'
pensions while wives of serving men are not taxed on their allowances.'

In 1954 Mr H. Morrison queried the position of First World War
widows in the proposed changes in war pensions as he had gathered
that many of them were having a very difficult time. He was assured
that they would benefit under the government proposals: 'Standard
rate for war widows with children or for widows over 40 years of

age will be raised from 42/- to 52/6 with appropriate increases for their children. War widows 1914–18 can be included in the above.' At this time the standard pension for a widow under the National Insurance scheme was 40s weekly. Again in December 1956 there were questions in the House as reported by Hansard: 'Rent allowance as the Hon gentleman knows – is payable only to war widows with children. The number of war widows over 40 years of age who are not eligible for this allowance is 135,000 of whom about 3,000 are in receipt of National Assistance.' In February 1957 a request that elderly war widows without children should be eligible for a rent allowance was denied.

> Even with National Assistance, this is not living, it is just existing, I am often cold and hungry.
> (Widow of lieutenant colonel, aged eighty)

> I have had to cut down on food this month to buy a much wanted pair of shoes. I have had to sell all my possessions and I have tried to get work but my age is against me.
> (Widow of lieutenant colonel, aged seventy-two)

Again, in the 1960 debate on the Queen's Speech, one Dr Wing pointed out that: 'War widows who receive a pension because they gave their husbands to the country have their pensions regarded for Income Tax as unearned income.'

MPs continued to highlight the plight of war widows from time to time but successive governments remained obdurate. In 1971 the matter was again raised by David Stoddard who pointed out that since war disability pensions were not taxed, why not exempt war widows' pensions as well. The widows themselves had no national organisation to fight for their interests and, because they did not speak with one voice, they could not put pressure on any government, be it Conservative or Labour. While war widows were duly appreciative of attempts made by individual MPs and others to improve their lot, their main grievance was taxation. The American allowances for war widows and their children were tax-free, and in Canada they received a flat-rate pension, with no distinction made for the rank of the late husband, again tax-free. Nor were war widows' pensions taxed in Australia and New Zealand. Britain was among the small minority of countries which did levy tax on such pensions – a tax which caused much bitterness among British war widows. One correspondent wrote that her mother was still paying tax in her seventies.

Two weeks after Betty Tebbs received the telegram telling her that her husband Ernest had been killed in France, a letter arrived from the Pensions Office informing her of her new circumstances. She would henceforth lose the Married Women's allowance of 28s per week, plus 12s 6d for her child. She would also lose the weekly 7s allowance that Ernest had sent her from his pay. She would now receive the basic War Widow's Pension of 26s 6d plus 11s weekly for her daughter. Now regarded as a single woman she would be taxed accordingly. This was a bitter blow for Betty who had the same commitments as she had before and was, at the same time, trying to cope with the loss of her husband. She felt abandoned by her country. Betty was working in a paper mill during the war and remembers feeling how grossly unfair it was that the married woman next to her on the production line paid no tax, in spite of living with her mother, having no home to maintain and no children and was still receiving her husband's army allowance.

This sense of what was felt to be discrimination against women already devastated by the fact of widowhood is reiterated by the following extracts from letters we have received:

I know that my mother was quite bitter about the fact that, on becoming a widow, all monies were withheld for several months. I have letters that she received (from military sources) confirming that my father had authorised payments to her before his death, and others promising to help if they could... Another sore point was that the pension was classed as 'unearned income'. In the 1950s my mother worked with women who were working for pin money. The weekly wage was £4. After paying a full stamp and income tax my mother's 'take home' pay was somewhat less than her colleagues who received the full £4.

I unfortunately lost my sailor husband, killed in action in 1943. Regarding then our meagre pension of £1 per week ... with no child and having to go out to work full time. The £1 was added in the Wage and became Taxed as Unearned Income which was 19 shillings, so that very little of the Pension was left. Our bank accounts could not increase very much in those circumstances and it meant living at home with our parents. No house of our own to look forward to.

My father was 'killed in action' in France on 22nd July 1944, he was 29, I was 3 years old. My mother never recovered from the shock of receiving the dreaded telegram and for the rest of her life suffered regular bouts of depression, no doubt made worse by the ever present shortage of money. Each year she would get an increase in her war widow's pension (pittance she always called it) there would be an almost similar increase in the council rent, she would say they give with one hand and take with the other. I would often come home from school to find her crying because she had just had a gas or electric bill or maybe I needed new shoes, and there was no money to pay… I have no complaint about my mother, she did her best under difficult circumstances but I do have issues with those organisations who should have helped…

My father was a PO subs [submarine service] off Crete in 1940 when he died. My mother was left with 4 children ages 14, 13, 10, 6; her income from Naval sources was £6, within 12 weeks it was £2/17/6d Her council rent was 12/6…

The constant niggardly approach to requests for benefits to which the young war widow was probably entitled on the face of it is almost beyond belief. In 1943 a war widow applied for free orange juice, cod liver oil and milk for her two young children. Children under five years old were eligible for these handouts to presumably give them a good nutritional base. Her application was refused because 'as there is only one parent living the maximum allowance for each non-earning is 27/6d plus 6d for each non-earning dependant. As your allowance is 41/6 (2/- above the maximum) your ration book is hereby returned.' She must have felt like weeping.

It was to address grievances such as this that finally led to the formation of the War Widows' Association in 1972. That the association was set up in 1972, some twenty-seven years after the end of the Second World War was due, ironically, to Laura Connolly, a war widow who had returned to England from Australia. Mrs Connolly had been accustomed to receiving a tax-free pension in Australia but on arriving in the mother country found her War Widow's Pension classed as unearned income and taxed accordingly. Informed that she would have to pay tax on her Australian pension of £11 per week, she refused. Eventually she owed the Inland Revenue £250 and faced bankruptcy proceedings but stoutly asserted: 'I did not have to pay tax on the pension in Australia. Then as soon as I set foot in England the authorities were on to me like a shot. I am not going to pay. There must be thousands of women throughout the country who feel as I do and we should band together to fight this unjust law.'

Her case and that of 'Britain's Forgotten Women' in general was enthusiastically taken up by the press and an article detailing her story was published in a Sunday newspaper in September 1971. It prompted another widow, Mrs F. Willis to write on 25 November to her local paper, the *Ruislip Gazette*:

Two weeks ago your paper published pages of what the British Legion does to help those affected by the Two World Wars. I and many other war widows are disappointed by the lack of effort by them regarding war widows' pensions. No other major country taxes war widows' pensions – not even Germany. Lord Mountbatten said at an ex-Serviceman's conference recently that it was painful the way successive governments treated war widows. The war has been over for over twenty-five years and I have not heard of any concerted effort by the British Legion to get this unfair tax abolished. War widows have now joined forces in their hundreds and are fighting to get this unfair tax abolished.

She also wrote to Laura Connolly:

> ... today (7th December) I went up to Westminster with the intention of seeing whether I could get into the public gallery of the House of Commons and shower a lot of leaflets down amongst the MPs ... the police told me they weren't sitting until 2.30 pm and as it was only about 10.45 am I couldn't hang about in the cold that long. I then went to No. 11 Downing Street and put some leaflets in the letter box, then did the same at No 10. Directly I did so the door opened. The policeman inside were also given leaflets and said they thought it terrible that we were taxed. The King of Afghanistan was given a State Drive through St James's Park to the Palace, so I went along the route giving out leaflets, which was good as there was a cross section of people... Not many people refused – in fact, some came up to me and asked for one... I have sent some leaflets to Wellington Barracks in London as the soldiers in Northern Ireland will come in for the same treatment if they are killed and leave wives and children...

It is not clear who produced the leaflets mentioned; perhaps Mrs Connolly herself was responsible. Her call to 'band together' triggered a flood of correspondence and the upshot was that fourteen women, coordinated by Jill Gee, a war widow from Liverpool, met in a Lyon's Cafe near the Houses of Parliament. They decided to form the WWA; its initial aim was to have the tax removed from the War Widow's Pension. The association was formally constituted in January 1972 with Jill Gee as Chairman, Denise Lorimer – the daughter of a war widow – as Secretary and Kathy Woodside, another widow, as Treasurer. Prior to the press publicity in 1971 not many people would have been aware of the plight of the war widow. Recognising the need for maximum impact in this, their first petition, the WWA sent out was a letter to all their supporters listing those publications which had spotlighted their campaign.

Letters and editorials of support had appeared in, among others, The Times, Liverpool Echo and Yorkshire Evening Post. Jill Gee was interviewed on the BBC 'PM' programme and sympathetic reports were aired by Manchester, Leeds and Merseyside radio stations. She also obtained an interview with the then minister of Health and Social Security, Sir Keith Joseph and wrote to Prime Minister Edward Heath. She was to write again and again to MPs, bombarding them with facts and contrasting the living standards of war widows in Britain with those in other countries. In Germany war widows were helped by a 2 per cent mortgage and in the USA with 5 per cent mortgages. Particularly galling to Mrs Gee was the treatment of war widows in Germany. Sufficient tax-free pensions to enable them to live comfortably without working, pensions calculated at an estimated 60 per cent of their deceased husband's assumed income and a free holiday every two years! Her communications were usually, as described by one MP, in 'the bitter and scathing tone at which Mrs Gee was so brilliant.'

By February 1972 the newly formed WWA was able to present a petition of 12,500 signatures to 10 Downing Street. The following letter is representative of the many letters which flooded into the WWA office:

With reference to the article re War Widows' pensions in the *Western Evening News* I should very much like to add my name to that Petition. I am a War Widow (Naval) my husband having been killed at Tobruk in 1942, and it has annoyed me for years to think that having made the supreme sacrifice, the Government then proceeded to take back part of that pension payable to the widow. Naturally I had to go back to work when I became a widow (one son) and always I have had to work for less than everybody else received, just because I was unfortunate [enough] to have lost my husband in the war. Right up to the end (I retired in 1970), although I earned more, I picked up less than the juniors of 16/17 years... Married women earning the same as me paid approx. £3 or £2.10/- [weekly] less than I did and they also had their husband's wages coming in... Even now I've retired I have had to pay about £84 tax this year... I am enclosing £1 with the hope that several other people will have the same idea and will send you enough to let you travel to London. Well, good luck anyway, any cause aiming to get this cruel tax removed would have my support. UNEARNED income they call [it]. My God, what more can a man do to earn it than give his very life!

This first petition was unsuccessful but the WWA was determined to continue the campaign. In September 1972 Jill Gee advised those writing to their MPs to point out that:

Our tax system is not based on the principle that the burden of tax be shared fairly and measured by total income and family commitments, i.e. married women do not have the 'commitment' of paying the rent, rates, food etc. yet no account is taken of this when allowing them to earn £592 FREE OF TAX. MPs and members of the House of Lords receive tax free incomes, yet there are apparently about 60 Peers who are millionaires...

Later, the aforementioned Iris Strange joined the organisation and became Secretary. In the 1950s she had asked her MP for help only to be told that there were thousands worse off than her, so to stop complaining. It was now Iris who dealt with the myriad letters to the WWA from the literally thousands of war widows. Joyce Maxwell, one of the founder members, described the War Widow's Pension as never sufficient to support a family 'except in the meagrest of fashions'. Was this the best the British government could do for the wives and children of the men who had died in the service of their country? From that small beginning by fourteen determined women, smarting under a great sense of injustice, the WWA has become a national association with Prince Charles as its patron, recognised, respected and with considerable influence.

The matter was meanwhile still being pursued in Parliament in 1975, this time in the House of Lords. Lord Clifford named fifteen countries besides the Commonwealth which did not tax widows' pensions. During the same debate Lord Blyton described the plight of a war widow with a pension of £11.10 (post decimalisation) per week, earning £7.10 in the school meals service, paying £5 a week for her council house with no rebate and having tax of £2.45

deducted from her income. He enquired: 'Does the Minister not think that something ought to be done in relation to tax for such people?' Again the answer was 'No', the Minister regretting that in the current economic circumstances he could do no more. Lord Maybray-King joined in the debate asking the Minister if he was aware that all the ex-servicemen's associations, while appreciating what successive governments had done for them, have placed in the forefront of their campaigns the widows of fallen comrades. The Minister gave a somewhat evasive reply at which Baroness Ward observed that war widows: 'Never had as much attention paid to their claims as they ought to have had, irrespective of whichever government was in power.' In May 1976 in reply to a question from Mr Kilroy-Silk, the Secretary of State for Social Services, Alfred Morris informed the House that at 31 December 1975, 90,276 war widows were in receipt of a pension. In response to a further question he said that war widows' pensions were treated as taxable income only in Holland, Norway, Denmark and Ireland.

The WWA never stopped lobbying Parliament for the removal of tax on their pensions. Dorothea Pullen has a vivid recollection of herself and Iris Strange going to the Houses of Parliament to plead their cause. Their efforts were eventually rewarded in 1976 when the Labour government reluctantly agreed to the removal of 50 per cent of the tax; the remaining 50 per cent being removed by the Conservative government of Margaret Thatcher in 1979. In February 1979 when the fight for the removal of the final 50 per cent tax was at its height the *Daily Express* printed the harrowing story of Mrs Elsie Evans:

Mrs Elsie Evans is dead. Her death is something of a relief. She was 80 years old. Virtually blind. Almost unable to walk or even move her neck. What little life was left in the pathetic old lady was steadily ground out of her by the inhumanity that only large government departments can show. Mrs Evans lived alone in a council flat in Coventry. As the widow of an RAF officer she received a pension. Although this was only a few pounds a week it meant that she could not claim Social Security. When her pension was raised to just over £6, the income tax man moved in and claimed £2.63; leaving her only £3.47. When she subsequently received an extra 53p the tax man moved in again and grabbed 52p. For Mrs Evans there was just one penny.

To this day Dorothea Pullen (writing in 2010) and many others remain very appreciative of Mrs Thatcher 'who took the tax off':

While the Labour Government was in there was nothing for war widows. My wages were added to the very small pension and taxed at thirty three and one third per cent. When Mrs Thatcher came on the scene Jill Gee, Iris Strange, myself and two other ladies – now dead – all went to the Houses of Parliament and pleaded our cause...

But there was more to come as the WWA then took up the cause of war widows who, at the age of sixty, found they were not entitled to a retirement pension, the government position being that if they had not paid National Insurance contributions they could not claim the State Pension. In 1980 Iris Strange, still Secretary of the WWA, maintained that the many women who had devoted most of their adult lives to nursing their war-disabled husbands had had no opportunity to work and pay the required contributions. She described it as 'monstrous' to declare that these women had not worked:

Many have worked night and day, ceaselessly, for years in order to keep their men at home rather than have them nursed in hospital. They worked as no nurse today would work. Many have never known the pleasure of an occasional holiday and all have shared the poverty of [the] war widow and the war disabled. It would be an enlightening exercise to work out how much money these women have saved the country between them in hospitalisation. About five years ago it was estimated that the cost per day for each hospital patient was £30.

She went on to highlight the plight of war widows who had been misinformed regarding their National Insurance contributions:

In the 1950s it became possible for some women to opt out of the payment of the full insurance stamp and to pay for the nominal stamp instead. Some were told by clerks at Labour Exchanges and others by personnel officers that no one is allowed to draw more than one State Pension and that they therefore [were] not be able to apply for a retirement pension because they already had a war widow's pension…

She then quoted from a letter she had received:

In 1972 the manager at the Ministry of Labour also told me that if I went on paying the full stamp I could [still] not expect to receive a pension, sickness benefit or unemployment benefit… That as I had a War Widow's pension I would not receive anything else, but I said as this was my sole idea of paying, then there was no purpose. Thus making myself ineligible for a pension in my own right when I'm 60 years. If only civil servants would get their facts right many would not be in the position of having to ask the DHSS for help, even if they don't receive it. Last winter I pleaded with the DHSS for help with heating bills; falling on deaf ears… For many years I have fought with the DHSS by letter and I shall continue to do so. However now they had better beware for I shall continue to inform Mr G. Jones MP at first hand, thus giving him more facts to use.

Despite the continuing efforts of Iris and others, all administrators stood firm and years later, in 1992 (which was to be the year of her death), she received a letter from the Prime Minister's secretary informing her that a special leaflet, NI 10, had been issued in January 1958 explaining important changes in the position of war widows. They had all been informed individually and there was coverage in the national press. He then reiterated the official position which is as difficult to comprehend now as it was then.

As far as retirement pensions are concerned, until 1958 war widows were required to pay National Insurance contributions. From 6 January that year a war widow could, provided she was in receipt of a pension equal to, or more than, the standard rate of National Insurance Widow's pension, choose not to pay contributions. It follows, therefore, that a widow who exercised this right would not have a full insurance record, and future entitlement to all benefits, including Retirement Pension, could be affected.

Iris went on to make the point that many countries have non-contributory retirement pensions for their war widows and that the obvious thing was to award all British war widows a retirement pension regardless of contributions. The official reply to that was that there might be an entitlement for women over eighty (subject to a simple residence test), to a non-contributory pension set at £32.55 weekly (60 per cent of the basic retirement pension). This was the usual cheeseparing parsimony for the few surviving elderly ladies who lost their husbands such a very long time ago.

Three

PENSIONS PARITY

THE FALKLANDS Conflict of 1982, when the Argentines tried to reclaim islands that they considered to be rightfully theirs, was short, sharp and, with victory, a great fillip for British morale. In the resultant outburst of generosity by the British public, the South Atlantic Fund, set up to aid the dependants of the 257 casualties incurred, raised £10 million. It was the largest sum ever raised by public subscription in this country. The fund's trustees announced that every woman widowed in the action would receive £10,000 from the fund and £1,000 would be given to every child whose father had died in the ten weeks of fighting. Thus the widow of a serviceman killed in the Falklands already had a pension double that of a Second World War widow (post-1973 classification) and in addition was to be given a tax-free lump sum. While the earlier widows did not begrudge these young women the increased pension and extra payments, they could not help but contrast their respective situations. They would not have been human if they had not felt, and articulated, some degree of bitterness:

> They worry if they have not had a letter for three weeks. My God, we waited three years for a letter and then when it came it was to say that he had died.

My husband died in Burma in 1944, but a woman whose husband was killed in the Falklands gets twice as much as me. I think it is scandalous the way we older ones, slowly growing fewer in number, are treated.

Is the sacrifice of one man's life for his country greater than that of another depending on the year it was given?

I had been married only three months when my husband was killed in World War 2. I brought up my daughter on a pension of only £3.50 a week. I can only hope that those who have lost loved ones because of the Falklands operation will be better treated than those of the past and receive every penny of the cash that is due to them.

... Widows are widows and the same no matter what the rank of their husbands or the circumstances in which they gave their lives for their country. There is an awful lot of ballyhoo being attached to the Falklands conflict and, without wishing to take anything from the lads, there were an awful lot of servicemen who did far more in totally worse conditions for years on end.

The ladies of the WWA could have expected that with the removal of income tax from their pensions their work was done, but they were to face yet another struggle. The campaign in Northern Ireland from 1973 and that in the Falklands in 1982 were to create a further group of war widows. In addition to the standard War Widow's Pension the Ministry of Defence decided to pay these widows of career servicemen a second pension (euphemistically described as an 'Occupational Pension') giving them a total amount worth more than double that paid to war widows of previous conflicts. In effect the widow of a private killed in the Falklands conflict received a basic £124 per week while a woman widowed in the Second World War was allotted a mere £57.

By 1982 Iris Strange had formed her breakaway organisation, the British War Widows and Associates (BWWA) which had approximately the same aims as the WWA but with a lot more cut and thrust. Many women belonged to both groups. When Iris first learned of the second pension she telephoned the Ministry of Defence to check the accuracy of the information. On ascertaining that it was correct she immediately entered the fray. In her BWWA newsletter of April 1982 she wrote:

> The second pension brings these widows' state incomes more into line with those of war widows in all other civilised countries, but a date on the calendar precludes all this country's war widows from receiving similar pensions. We do not begrudge these young widows their more realistic incomes but we do complain that, after a lifetime of abject poverty, we are not accorded the same extra pension. We consider that bearing in mind that our husbands laid down their lives for the freedom of this country, we are entitled to a similar income.

She now organised petitions using her nationwide contacts. One male supporter wrote her the following letter in 1984:

> When I wrote to the Prime Minister some time ago I had a reply in which she boasted about how much the present government had done for war widows and seemed almost indignant that I should write on their behalf. The letter from the Ministry of Defence is the usual put-off. No money, yet they can pour money into Fortress Falklands etc. You may remember that about two years ago the government granted a payment of £2,000 to a self-confessed IRA man, as compensation for having his lorry searched. It does not pay to be a law-abiding citizen nowadays... Would you let me have half a dozen sheets for signatures as the one I have now is almost full.

Iris' reply in typically robust fashion also illustrates her intense commitment to the cause. All correspondence is typewritten as far as we can judge, by Iris herself, and many of the letters are inordinately long:

> I agree with all you say. Members of Parliament, particularly Ministers do brag about what they are supposed to have done for us. Thank you

for mentioning payment of £2,000 to the IRA man: I had not heard about it and I collect snippets of information of that nature which make interesting reading and useful 'ammunition'. The £180 million which it would cost to pay us the second pension is a very tiny sum compared to other amounts bandied about in Government circles for less important things. I took part in a Radio Bristol programme where I was able to tell listeners that a government spokesman had suggested to Parliament paying unemployed 'layabouts' £60 a week each if they reported to, and remained in, day centres during working hours and stopped mugging people. I pointed out that there are more of that category than there are war widows and that we are asking for less than £60 a week each. I was followed on the programme by Mr Anthony Beaumont-Dark MP who agreed with everything I said and declared that the sum stated (£180 million to pay the second pension) was very small in Government terms and concluded by saying 'this is money we cannot afford not to afford'.

I must thank you for all your support. Those in high places take little notice of war widows because we are a fast-dying section of the community but they become very jumpy indeed when other people join us in our fight for justice. We shall only win with the support of those who are not war widows.

From bitter experience the vast majority of war widows were only too well aware that parity of pensions could only be achieved through Parliamentary legislation. As is illustrated by this extract from Hansard there were many sympathetic MPs in the House. In 1985 Geoffrey Dickson MP made a speech in which he declared:

It can never be denied that we owe an enormous debt of honour to all the widows of those who fell in the service of their country in the First and Second World Wars. Indeed without their supreme sacrifice Hon Members of this house would not have the privilege of serving in a freely elected Parliament. Today's war widows have security and care, but not so the widows of the two World Wars... This country has betrayed British war widows of two World Wars.

Nicholas Winterton, the MP for Macclesfield, had also spoken in the House on their behalf and Iris Strange approached him with the idea of forming an all-party group within Parliament to lobby for parity for the pre-1973 war widows. This he did with enthusiasm, appealing for war widows to supply him with the relevant information, although there was still to be no quick fix. This letter was one of those he received in answer to his request:

> During the war I worked on munitions in South Wales. A short time before my husband's death (he was 100 per cent disabled) we applied for National Assistance and were granted one shilling and sixpence weekly. My husband wrote and told them to keep it. I was widowed in 1950 and granted a war widow's pension of £2/18/6d a week, out of that amount I had to pay rent and rates and provide for myself and my young son. Life was very hard and difficult. During the summer months I took in paying guests, in winter I did sewing work in my home. When my son started school I went out and did part-time work; anything I could get that enabled me to be with my son after school hours and keep the wolf from the door. At present I am living with him and his family and try as far as possible to share the household expenses. In fact I am depending on him for a roof over my head, otherwise I would not be able to exist on my war pension as I have no other income. I am most grateful and thankful to you for your interest in the welfare of war widows...

The WWA also took up the fight for equal pensions for all war widows. They were to campaign ceaselessly, writing letters to newspapers and politicians, presenting their case on radio and television in what was virtually a repeat of the fight for the removal of tax on the pension. This time the Officers' Pension Society worked with the WWA forming the Campaign for Equal Pensions for War Widows and getting a lot of support from well-known personalities such as Vera Lynn and BBC journalist and agony aunt Anna Raeburn. In 1986 the *Liverpool Daily Post* reported that an anonymous benefactor had enabled the BWWA to engage a barrister, Steve Grosz, to fight the case for equal pensions for all war widows. Mr Grosz investigated the possibility of taking the case to the European Commission of Human Rights but reported that there was no chance of success. There was a lot of encouragement from the public. This example from the Iris Strange Collection dated 9 February 1988 and from an ex-serviceman writing to his MP Kenneth Hargreaves, pulls no punches:

> I would like to express my thanks to you for exposing the plight of our War Widows in your talk on the 'Members Only' programme, Granada T/V Sunday Jan 31st. The shabby and contemptible way in which these unfortunate ladies have [been] treated is shameful in the extreme and borders on criminal negligence, a fact that is made more apparent when compared to their European counterparts. Speaking as an ex-serviceman I feel very bitter and disillusioned that we as a nation can allow this inexcusable situation to continue when their husbands have made the supreme sacrifice. They must be wondering if they would not have been better off if the Germans had won the war.
>
> The only three things which successive governments have achieved in the last forty years are 'Absolutely, Bloody, Nothing'. Their efforts being about as much use as a one-legged man in an arse-kicking contest. These Widows from the last war are now at an age when they are no longer able to work to supplement their pensions... If this letter is passed on to the Minister concerned, I would like to say to him, for God's sake give them what they deserve now, that they may have some comforts in their remaining days...

The Times printed a strong letter of support from Admiral of the Fleet Lord Hill-Norton and other prominent service chiefs:

> The war widows of this country have been forgotten for too long; their own sacrifice unacknowledged. When men are asked to give their lives for their country, they have to believe that their wives and children will be adequately provided for and servicemen are, understandably, more concerned for their dependants than themselves. Indeed this was the reason for the improvement in that aspect of Service pensions in 1973. However to improve the pensions of one small group of younger war

widows, while continuing to ignore the financial and emotional hardships of over 95% (who represent our older war widows) is an unjust
and cruel blow. Their patient suffering, resilience and determination
to get on with life, whilst being both mother and father to their children has condemned many of them to an existence on the edge of the
poverty line ... we call on this Government to remove the artificial
wall – March 31 1973 – which divides our war widows into first and
second-class citizens.

The nationwide campaign grew even louder and more insistent
and in July 1988 a war widow from Wales composed this impassioned letter to Mrs Thatcher:

When you became Prime Minister I had high hopes that, at last, war
widows would receive sympathetic treatment. On your recent visit to
the scene of the Piper Alpha disaster [an oil rig fire off the Scottish coast],
you showed your deep concern by donating a million pounds of tax-
payers' money toward the Relief Fund. Your action has set me thinking. I
heard your reply – P.M. Questions, House of Commons – to a question
about the plight of many war widows. You stated, very emphatically, that
'this government has been more generous than any previous government towards war widows' ... You referred to the removal of income
tax from our pensions. It was a Labour government which made the first
move. They cut the tax by 50% so it was very politic of you to honour
your promise to end the other 50% liability... Many war widows who,
for good reasons were unable to take jobs, received no benefit from this
move. In my own case during the years between 1943, when my husband was killed in action, and 1964 I had to work very hard to provide
for my two sons. Our pension was a mere pittance, a total of £178 a year.
During those long and lonely years of sacrifice, I paid income tax at the
single person's rate, even though I had all the responsibilities of the head
of a family. The whole of my war widow's pension, and a part of my
salary were cancelled out by income tax.

As you would know, up to the year 1973, all World War II widows'
pensions were administered by a single scale. It was the introduction
of the Forces' Families Pension which has caused my resentment.

I consider that my husband's life was given in order that all the people of this country could live in freedom, and receive equally fair treatment from the state. I do not accept that service, either in Northern Ireland or for a few months in the Falklands, justifies preferential treatment with regard to war pensions.

The men who work on North Sea Oil Rigs know of the danger involved when they take on their jobs, they accept it in return for very high pay. Their dependants will receive very high insurance payments and compensation from their employers in addition to good pensions. So, please, when you distribute largesse from this country's great resources, would you remember all those people whose lives were shattered by two <u>World Wars?</u> They have lived in poverty ever since. Whatever you might wish to subscribe towards Piper Alpha [disaster], as a private person, is not my concern. I would remind you that our numbers are falling, you would not be required to pay our pensions for more than a decade. Also that, however high any award might be made to us at this late date, it could never make up for the heartless treatment meted out to our fatherless children all those sad years ago...

As the situation dragged on many of the early war widows began to despair; they felt they had to fight for every small scrap thrown at them, for example the government agreeing to make an annual sum available to the Royal British Legion (RBL) to assist women to visit their husbands' graves overseas. In the same year the government acknowledged that women widowed after 1973 did receive a pension double that of the earlier widows but ascribed the 'discrepancy' as arising purely because of improvements in the Family Forces Pension Scheme of April 1973. To remove the 'discrepancy' would breach a long-standing principle of pension schemes: there are no retrospective payments. It would also have cost about £200 million annually. (The cost of granting parity varies according to the source. Iris Strange estimated £180 million with which the RBL concurred. Government figures varied widely, or rather, wildly between £600 million and, later, in 1989, £110 million.)

Another letter in the archive is from a lady in Cornwall, obviously very distressed:

I wrote to David Steele [leader of the Liberal Party], also Margaret Thatcher, she didn't reply, the letter came from the D[epartment] of the E[nvironment] who pay the second pension to war widows. When I read it, it made my blood boil. They cannot afford to pay us war pensions as it would cost too much yet they give themselves a £4,000 rise. David Steele's letter sounds a bit more hopeful… It's really scandalous – hope I've spelt that right – how we older widows are treated … I sat down the other day and cried, thinking why did my husband have to be killed [for me] to be treated like this. £4,000 would do us for years… My rent is now £114-odd a month, and it is up again in April. I just couldn't pay it so will find a cheaper rent. When the Poll Tax comes in goodness knows what I will pay, sometimes it seems that life isn't worth living these days but we have to keep going.

In 1987 a member from Northern Ireland put her view to the WWA:

As a war widow, have you ever applied to the DHSS for help? If not let me tell you I would rather starve; help may be available for the ordinary widow but not for the war widow in receipt of such a 'high pension'. When I look [around] and see some widows of part-time servicemen murdered here and consider how well they are catered for by the government; two pensions and, from the Ulster Defence Benevolent Association two weeks free holiday each summer, bus outings, Christmas Dinners etc. Not that I begrudge them one penny. I ask myself why should I, a war widow who has struggled and worked hard to rear my son, have to go begging to the DHSS to ask for clothing etc.? For the past few years I have received a gift of coal from a charity but had to complete a questionnaire and state the allowance I make to my son for my keep. I was also asked if I had any savings. If so, state how much. If the only advice the Association can give is 'go and ask' I prefer to go without.

The all-party group increased their pressure on the government and in March 1989 Frank Dobson MP contested the government figures pointing out that as more and more of the pre-1973 widows were dying out the government were already saving £20 million a year on pensions they no longer had to pay out. He then went on to disclose that when Mrs Thatcher was leader of the opposition, two letters had been sent from her office on her behalf supporting parity, one in 1975 and another in 1978. He quoted from the latter:

> I quite accept that the present situation is unsatisfactory and Mrs Thatcher has agreed that it is now our wish to establish as rapidly as economic circumstances will allow a scheme whereby the widows of all servicemen killed in action (or dying from causes attributable to active service) would receive a pension to that now awarded to widows of servicemen currently in the armed forces.

He added:

> Clearly the time has come for the Prime Minister to honour her promise. She cannot argue that economic circumstances do not permit the Government to find the money because she constantly boasts how prosperous the country is these days. We have been told that the Chancellor proposes to use some of his Budget surplus to pay off the national debt. Surely he should pay off our national debt to war widows. There is no group to whom our nation owes a greater debt.

The government remained intransigent, reiterating that changes to pension schemes could not be retrospective and claiming that by fully removing the tax from war widows' pensions they had done more to help them than any other administration. But the all-party Parliamentary campaign, headed as mentioned by Nicholas Winterton, was by now nigh-on unstoppable and in July 1989 he replied to one correspondent:

At a recent meeting with the Select Committee for Social Services, of which I am the longest serving Member of Parliament, the Minister of State, Nicholas Stott MP made the claim that although he had offered to consider carefully any cases of hardship among war widows he had HAD NOT ONE SINGLE CASE REFERRED TO HIM FOR CONSIDERATION since he made the offer. I am determined that he will not be able to use this excuse for inaction in the future and I undertake to refer personally to the Minister every single case of hardship which is referred to me, so that the next time I have the opportunity to question him through the Select Committee he will be fully aware of the real plight of pre-1973 war widows. If you know of any other war widows who are facing difficult circumstances then please ask them to write [to me] as well.

In November of that year Alfred Morris MP, opposition spokesman for Social Services, whose own mother had been a war widow deprived of any pension at all, issued a clarion call to Parliament:

The fundamental issue is about settling a debt, not just of gratitude but of honour to the widows of the men who gave their lives for this country before the Armed Forces Pension Scheme took effect in 1973... The issue is not one that divides Conservative Members from Opposition Members. The divide is between most Members from both sides of both Houses of Parliament and the Government. A clear majority of this House supported the early day motion calling for equal provision for all war widows. With 350 signatories, it became the most widely supported motion of this Parliament, and many more Members would have signed had they not been debarred from doing so by the position they hold. To their honour we are also backed tonight by forthright campaigning in the media as a whole. Like the vast majority of the British people the media insist that equality of treatment for the pre-1973 war widows is now an urgent imperative.

On 11 December 1989 the government capitulated. The Secretary for Defence, Mr Tom King, stated that the government recognised the great strength of feeling shown by members of both Houses and by so many of the general public in support of the pre-1973 war widows. He reaffirmed the position taken by the government that any improvements to the existing pension scheme could not be applied retrospectively. The government now proposed to give the pre-1973 widows an additional payment of £40 per week – entirely free of tax – to be implemented in April 1990.

Many war widows were understandably sceptical but in her BWWA newsletter of January 1990 Iris Strange was able to reassure them:

> We really will be having a £40 EXTRA added to our war pension from April 9th. More good news is that it is not to be taxed, nor is it to be allowed to lessen housing benefits. A number of members have telephoned me and others have written, full of scepticism about this and are waiting to find out how the government are going to claw some, or all of it, back, but I can assure everyone that it really is extra and no deductions whatsoever are to be made.

Of the 212,427 war widows alive in 1945 only 52,713 were left to benefit from this bonanza.

Four

THE ROLE OF THE BENEVOLENT SOCIETIES

A **S WE** have seen, the pension structure was less than perfect and in any event too many widows fell through the gaps, notably the wives of men posted 'missing' and not confirmed prisoner of war for perhaps months, or even years. This was also the situation initially for the dependants of merchant seamen who customarily signed on for the one voyage and who were not tied into any pension scheme, and the widows of civilians working for the military who fell into no category except perhaps that of the '10s widow' (the weekly sum paid to a childless widow of an insured person under the 1935 Act). Sometimes surprisingly there were also problems for the widows of servicemen who died of natural causes or accidents. 'No war pension was ever paid due to the assertation [sic – assertion] by his Commanding Officer that his [father's] death was by natural causes.'

To whom did the widow appeal for assistance, temporary or otherwise? One widow was told that one of the ways to get something from the benevolent societies was to run up a debt which one of the charitable associations would be more likely to clear, though we found no particular examples of this practice. The benevolent organisation which most people first think of is the British Legion (now the Royal British Legion) founded in the early 1920s and still going strong. Its prime function was – as it is now – to campaign for the interests of ex-servicemen and women. These days most people associate it with the annual

Poppy Appeal, which raises a vast amount of money and funds the Legion rest homes, aids to the disabled and special grants etc. The numerous branches countrywide have two main objectives: a) to raise and distribute funds locally and b) to point applicants in the right direction; the latter is mostly the job of an unpaid local case worker. The local committees consist entirely of volunteers; only the headquarters staff and regional officers are paid.

Over the years, the job of actually handing out relief to veterans and their dependants seems to have shuffled between the local committees and the regional office. For example at the meeting of the Shelford branch in November 1942 the Secretary reported the 'recall of all moneys held by the local Committee' and that any assistance would 'henceforth be made from the Regional Office'. The administration of funds has also changed with time and payments from area funds, invariably piecemeal, were usually made to the war veterans themselves in the form of sickness grants, money for food, coal and rent etc. The local branches could also step in and give immediate assistance while a widow's claim for a pension was going through the various stages. One lady in 1942 received £1 weekly for four weeks to tide her over. A laughable sum these days but then it was probably a life saver. The Shelford branch also agreed to cover the expenses of a war widow needing treatment at a specialist clinic in Droitwich at 'area's expense' and in 1949 the committee apparently distributed Australian food parcels to '5 War Widows, ex area'. Many local branches still hold a small welfare fund to deal with modest requests for immediate assistance such as a financial contribution towards a wheelchair.

But to what extent was their help immediate and generous especially in the post-war years when it was vital? The British Legion's monthly magazine is a very good source of its activities as long as one bears in mind that obviously they are not going to print anything that would reflect badly on them. In February 1944 they successfully fought the case of the widow of a forty-three-year-old member of the Home Guard who died of a heart attack not while he was on duty but following a stressful fourteen-day military camp. The lady was awarded £1 6s 8d weekly

for life. In the same month, the Executive Council protested the
long delays – often some six months – before a widow could have
her case heard by the pensions tribunals; a delay during which she
would have no income whatsoever. In 1945 the Executive Council
declared that: 'No war widow should be forced to go out to work,
it was argued, if she had a home and children to look after.' In
1965, 450 widows were receiving allowances (not specified) at
a cost to the Legion of £11,691. Plans were also announced for
a block of twenty-one flats to be built at Westgate-on-Sea for ex-
servicemen or widows thereof. Notably in 1966 a party consisting
of forty war widows and some 100 of their children were given
a fortnight's holiday by the sea at Burnham-on-Sea in Somerset,
accommodated in 'luxury chalets' at Brean Sands holiday camp
and only having to pay for their food. One recipient later thanked
the Legion for 'my first holiday in 11 years'.

The Royal British Legion Housing Association was formed in
1964 and twenty years later it catered for 15,000 residents, pre-
dominantly ex-service. At the RBL complex at Aylesford there were
eighty housing units in the 1980s. The funding for these projects
was sometimes government controlled rather than exclusively
RBL. There were also convalescent homes such as that at Weston-
super-Mare where a disabled veteran and family could have a
break. Aside from the RBL Industries Village at Aylesford there
are other training sites: a Security Control and Training Centre
was opened in London in 1988. These undertakings are presumably where most of the money from the annual Poppy Appeal is
spent. There is a mention of small business loans and – again in
the 1980s – allowances of £4 weekly were paid to permanently
incapacitated widows. Specifically for the war widow there was a
Pilgrimage Department which handled the applications for visits
to overseas military cemeteries, the government bearing seven
eighths of the cost.

At the local level any distribution of funds was down to the
RBL committee and their interpretation of guidelines. One of our
respondents writes: 'Mother only received humiliation when she
once asked the British Legion for help'; another wrote: 'Mum

did write to the British Legion but never received anything' and 'Mother went to the British Legion for some kind of help and was told to go find a job – with 4 children under 5!' Another: 'I asked for 7/6 for essential dental treatment and was turned down outright.' One of the Mass Observation diarists quoted in Simon Garfield's *Our Hidden Lives* makes a rather surprising entry for 11 November 1945: 'I have no time for all this Legion annual nonsense – if ever a body was corrupt the British Legion is the one ... more than time it was investigated and exposed and finished.' It is probably true to say that between the wars the British Legion at local level was invariably chaired by the ranking First World War officer, usually a colonel, and that his committee was customarily landed gentry or members of one of the professions. Typically in 1987 the Legion reported an award handed to an ex-colonel after twenty-one years as chairman of his local branch. The Stapleford committee, for example, was chaired by local landowner Sir Harold Gray and on that committee were the local vicar and the doctor. One assumes that the diarist must have crossed swords with just such a committee at some point. No further explanation is offered. However, equally negative sentiments are expressed in the following letters from the Iris Strange archive:

> I am afraid the British Legion in Britain have not been of great help to war widows. Even with those war widows evicted from their homes they say they cannot help unless the war widow is over sixty...
> (January 1973)

> What you have told me about the lack of interest of the British Legion does not surprise me. Your complaint is one of hundreds I have received during past years, and my own personal experience of them was appalling...
> (December 1982)

> It might have been different if we'd had some help from the British Legion.

The furore created by the affair of the Dutch handouts is interesting and certainly does not present the RBL in a good light.
On the face of it, it seems to be a lot of fuss about nothing, but
sensibilities were hurt on all sides. It was also leaked to the press
and seemingly caused a lot of bitterness. It all began with a pilgrimage in November 1986 to Venvray in Holland by a group of
war widows, organised by the redoubtable Iris Strange and at the
invitation of the Dutch Veteran Association to visit the graves of
the 800 British soldiers buried there. The Dutch were immensely
hospitable and were apparently appalled by what they learnt of
the impecunious state of some of the women who lacked warm
winter clothing, and as a consequence, gifts came flooding in. As
one Dutchman later wrote: '... the radio and newspapers spent
[a lot of] attention to these spontaneous reactions resulting in a
stream of offerings, winter coats and money.' Reports must have
appeared in the British press, for in the May/June issue of the
Legion an article appeared stating categorically that the Dutch had
been 'misled' and setting out bona fide pension rates for war
widows: 'The Legion has been in direct touch with the Dutch
organisations whose local representatives have been so misled
and misguided.'

The flow of correspondence continued for months afterwards
and a solicitor's letter went to the WWA after an article appeared
in *Courage*, the newsletter of the WWA (quoting the above) which
defamed Iris Strange. This does not appear to have been pursued.
Many individuals and organisations did rush to Iris' defence and
in the archive are several press articles in support; perhaps she did
not keep the unfavourable ones!

A letter from one widow Mrs Beryl James to the General
Secretary of the RBL is particularly apt in the circumstances:

(26 June 1987)
... When I read your article I wonder whose side you are on. If
the article represents the policy of the Royal British Legion I thank
God for women like Mrs Iris Strange and men like Mr Nicholas
Winterton MP... I consider that Mrs Iris Strange has, single-handed,

done more than any ex-service welfare organisation to rally support for our cause...

Interestingly the Southend breakaway branch of the Far East
Prisoners of War Association (FEPOW) leapt to her defence,
and the following is an extract from a letter to Iris from their
Chairman: 'I am not a member of the Royal British Legion. Few
of us are, and I would emphasise that they do not represent all ex-
servicemen of this country.' Another widow writing in September
1988 was a member of both the WWA and an associate member
of the RBL: 'I maintain if the Legion was doing their work properly there would be no need for any other associations.'

The problems always seemed to be due to personality clashes,
for throughout the entire hullabaloo it is the RBL in Holland
together with the WWA who are handling the shipment and distribution of all the gifts collected by the generous Dutch people.
A WWA member in Northern Ireland was bemused by the WWA's
attitude to the whole affair – could any publicity be detrimen-
tal? As a postscript, the following letter to the WWA from another
member of both the WWA and the BWWA is interesting;

(20 June 1987)

You say you have had letters from all over the country complaining of
humiliation. I should think the cause for humiliation lies in the unfortunate headlines in the Sunday newspapers. I cannot see why generous
gifts given in a spirit of gratitude should be more humiliating than
having to go cap in hand to beg assistance from either the DHSS or the
Royal British Legion. Both these bodies are capable of refusing... If
one act of charity is humiliating, then so are all the others.

Every sizeable branch of the RBL publishes its own reports of res-
olutions, undertakings and activities from time to time. There are
also regional and national conferences on a much larger scale. A
resolution carried by the National Conference at Blackpool in May
1980 is quite categorical in support of the claim for parity of war
widows' pensions and notably concluded that: 'This conference

feels that all future Royal British Legion conferences should invite representatives of the War Widows' Association of Great Britain to attend conference.' A great improvement on Iris Strange's criticism that when the WWA was in its infancy:

> We thought the obvious place to start with was the RBL but to our astonishment they had no knowledge or data about war widows, nor of how their conditions compared with the widows of other countries...

In the postbag of the *Scottish Legion News* is a letter from a Korean War veteran regarding the 1973 pension anomalies:

> Far be it from me – a miserable ex-National Serviceman – to presume to tell RBSL their job, but is it not time that they stopped putting all their faith in passing Motions at Annual General Meetings, and instead started to Fight the Good Fight for a return to Equal Compensation for the Nation's War Disabled and War Widows.

There are indeed also many examples of the help arranged by the British Legion in individual cases. Bill Thompson writes that his father died of natural causes while a serving soldier and: 'No War Widows' pension was ever paid in spite of all efforts by the British Legion.' Janet Stubbins' mother (whose story was recounted earlier) also fell through the gap when her husband was knocked down by a car and killed in the blackout. He had spent thirty-six hours in the water at Dunkirk, and as a result was deaf in one ear and did not hear the vehicle approaching. Mrs Pople was informed that as he was killed off duty there would be no pension. Mrs Stubbins writes that the head of the local branch – one Captain Harper – worked tirelessly on her mother's behalf and managed to obtain an allowance from 'the local Parish charity' and a War Widow's Pension of 26s 6d per week finally came through after a two-year campaign. A mixed bag it would seem, and still these days very dependent on a case worker's assessment, married to the spider web of Social Services. Nowadays the RBL is principally associated with the Poppy Appeal; the membership is declining fast as the veterans of the Second World

War peter out and – fortunately – there is no longer a vast pool of ex-servicemen seeking social contact with their contemporaries.

The Royal Naval Benevolent Trust (RNBT) was another possible source of support. Founded in 1916, it was Admiral Jellicoe who initially proposed a charitable fund. The trust received a substantial boost when the Admiralty came up with £61,700 in 1922 and in the following years derived a large income from canteen profits. Roy Pickard recalls that the trust refused his mother a grant for a new suit for him but did offer to send him to a Naval orphanage. Elizabeth Knowling's widowed grandmother got a job as a Naval tailor but needed new glasses to cope: 'She approached the Naval Benevolent Fund to ask if they could help but was told she should sell her wireless in order to pay for the glasses.' She never asked for help again. The RNBT wrote a letter of condolence to Mrs Woodcock in 1941 offering what help they could with the proviso that they could not offer permanent assistance nor 'make grants towards the provision of mourning'. However Margaret Hothi whose father drowned when HMS *Royal Oak* was sunk at Scapa Flow in October 1939 recalls that the family did receive some help from the RNBT. For the widows of merchant seamen a Merchant Navy Welfare Board has been in existence more or less since 1937. Mostly known for the establishment of Seamen's Missions at home and abroad, its remit did include provision – financial and educational – for widows and dependants.

There was also of course an Army Benevolent Fund founded under the aegis of King George VI in August 1944. The structure is probably much the same as the British Legion, with area committees. Since 1964 serving soldiers have been encouraged to contribute one day's pay per annum to the fund which gives support in the form of housing, supplementary allowances, educational bursaries, holiday schemes and the like to veterans and their dependants. Interestingly the Army Widows' Association is apparently only concerned with women whose husbands died after 1981. There are still considerable numbers of regimental and corps associations all with much the same aims, such as the Royal Air Force Benevolent Fund, in existence since 1919. One of our respondents who had been in the WAAF herself was five months' pregnant when her husband was killed:

> My sister was still a serving officer in the WAAF... I went into 'digs' near where she was stationed and the RAF Benevolent Fund paid, and also for my confinement in a private nursing home. They then found me various 'house-sitting' jobs...

Now, everything is on a much larger scale than during the immediate post-war period with which we are probably most concerned. In 2009 the Army Benevolent Fund donated £750,000 towards housing for veterans.

Apart from the RBL, the Soldiers', Sailors' and Airmen's Families Association (SSFA until 1919, SSAFA thereafter) is probably the most all encompassing. Founded over a hundred years ago it does mirror the RBL in many respects and their decisions too seem to be arbitrary. It is difficult to discover how funds are distributed and these days the two organisations do appear to be interconnected; for instance they will co-operate to fund an expensive item such as a stair lift. SSAFA also run homes for veterans and are often subsidised by other charities. In wartime the organisation covered a vast area, literally and figuratively, running marriage guidance bureaux in the Middle East, counselling in hospitals and troop depots, etc and even assisting unmarried pregnant servicewomen by providing the layette. Most of our examples come from the pre-NHS late 1940s and the early 1950s. In one case SSAFA refused to pay the 7s 6d needed for a child's visit to the doctor but did later help the widow of an RAF sergeant with her house repairs. Mrs Ball recalls that the SSAFA paid her £7 when her son started school and again when he was seven years old; another widow got 6s for her child for a mere four weeks. Janet Pople apparently received a grant of £5 quarterly from the Stars and Stripes War Orphans' Fund – the grand sum of £100 in all – which was latterly distributed by SSAFA. There are occasional references to the SSAFA helping out, though very minimally, with uniform costs when a son or daughter got into a grammar school.

This is not to denigrate the very valuable work done by the SSAFA in recent years, much of it on a large scale. To celebrate its 125th anniversary in 2010 for example, a sky diving event was planned with 125 prospective 'jumpers' paying £75 each. The association also sponsored runners in the London Marathon. These days it is a far-reaching comprehensive organisation, with each county having paid caseworkers to help servicemen and ex-servicemen and their dependants to '... seek grants from Service, Regiment and other funds or assist in seeking grants elsewhere...' (in 2010 they advertised 1,413 job vacancies nationwide).

In our sample some widows received help from their husband's former employers such as the example previously quoted where the family were allowed to stay on in the miner's cottage. The chocolate manufacturers Cadbury paid the bus fares when one widow's daughter went to grammar school and sent a box of chocolates every Christmas. Gifts at Christmas are also given by such organisations as the Fire Service and the Mechanics' Union. Occasionally there is a reference to assistance from the Parish or Church but most would have done anything rather than go 'on the Parish' a term of denigration at the time. Carol Woodward's mother felt compelled to apply to the Public Assistance Board only to be turned down because her children were 'clean in body and clothing'. Strangely only one of the seventy plus people who replied to our questionnaire mentioned the Church, or indeed religion, as being of help at a difficult period. Obviously some support was forthcoming from other sources; one family received grants for school uniform from the Royal Antediluvian Order of Buffaloes.

Another organisation, whose green uniforms would have been familiar to everybody during the war itself, was the Women's Voluntary Service (WVS) founded by Stella Marchioness of Reading in 1938 to deal with the exigencies of the coming war, '... mobilising resources of over a million women by 1942...'. It was the WVS who endlessly stepped into the breach, handing out cups of tea and blankets after air raids and helping the troops returning from Dunkirk, etc. Principally middle-class ladies of

leisure, they were not, however, happy to welcome the hoi polloi
into their midst: 'I remember my mother's offer of help being
turned down; she was not quite the right type!' Most of these
ladies however did a sterling job, helping with emergency housing, soup kitchens and running second-hand clothing exchanges
that were an absolute boon to anyone with small children. The
Salvation Army too was often there to pick up the pieces and fill
the gaps; many people remember their help with gratitude, especially in wartime.

What they – the children – all do remember is the joy with
which they received parcels from abroad, particularly from the
American, Canadian and Australian Red Cross. Janet Stubbins was
'adopted' by the American Red Cross and still recalls the contents
of the parcel she got that first Christmas after her father's death:

> 2 dollies, 2 books, a box of Black Magic chocolates, many packets of
> sweets, a box of handkerchiefs, tablets of soap and several games and
> a pack of cards. I was absolutely stunned, I thought I was in heaven...

Janet also recalls one Christmas when an envelope containing
a £1 note was pushed through the letterbox by an anonymous
donor, thus ensuring that the family could both get the radio
repaired and have a chicken for Christmas dinner! Gift parcels
were somewhat hit and miss but always remembered: 'We had a
parcel from Canada and my sister and I were very excited when
we saw a Tate & Lyle syrup tin – but it contained dripping.' 'My
brother and I received a book each from Canada, mine was *Pride
and Prejudice* and his was *Gulliver's Travels*. I believe these were sent
from the *Toronto Evening News* and I still have mine.' One girl had an
American foster parent who made regular monthly donations,
while others received parcels of clothing. Nora Lestrange writes
that in 2009 she still had the tin of honey sent from Australia –
nobody liked honey!

Solely based on our findings it would seem that the disparate
benevolent societies and charities suffered variously from the
same drawbacks as the pension scheme; the aid given was so often

a matter of interpretation or whim. This may have had something to do with the fact that so many of the volunteers who gave so much of their time and energy were enthusiastic amateurs. It is estimated that there were some 10,000 charities at large by 1945 collecting and distributing and probably often treading on each other's toes. A large number of these, possibly the majority, were not registered under the War Charities Act and some of them were certainly scams. Nonetheless the legitimate charitable organisations have done valuable work over the years but have sometimes failed to give help to those most in need of it; in this instance the war widow and her children.

Five

A DIFFERENT LIFE –
COPING WITH WIDOWHOOD

WHEN CONSIDERING this chapter it must be pointed out that there would have been, especially in recent years, many women widowed by the Second World War who would not have answered any request such as ours. 'What does it matter now after all these years?' would be a very understandable reaction. Time and time again those who did respond questioned why they weren't given more support earlier when they were so desperately in need. More support from successive governments, more support from the benevolent societies, more understanding from the general public and from other women in the same situation. For unlike war widows in some Commonwealth countries (in Australia the War Widows' Guild dates from 1945) there was no centralised support structure in this country until 1971, partly because post-war governments until then refused to release the name of war widows. There were areas however – particularly at the ports – where the spouses of men missing or killed gathered to support each other. In Plymouth a War Widows' Guild was formed in 1945, at the instigation of the head of the local Community Services Council, which did give the widows of Naval personnel some small comfort.

After VJ Day government departments published a plethora of pamphlets giving help and advice to returning servicemen. The War Office, the Ministry of Labour and assorted charities offered help to former POWs, while couples facing problems after perhaps six years of wartime separation were given marriage guidance, but official help did not seem to extend to war widows. The only advice and somewhat limited support came from the voluntary organisations such as the Salvation Army, the Royal British Legion and the Church. As one put it: 'As a young war widow I was among the ranks of the "walking wounded". Almost ignored as if one had a dread disease no-one wanted to know about.' In her book *The Anatomy of Bereavement* Beverley Raphael lists the stages following bereavement from initial numbness, through grief, to anger and then loneliness; the first six weeks being the most painful followed by acute distress in the next few months. She points out that anniversaries trigger a reoccurrence of the intense grief and that if there is a child the widow will try harder to control her feelings. Friends and relatives often keep their distance for fear of being too involved emotionally or financially as is illustrated by the above comment. Was it any different being a war widow?

During the war itself the tension must have been unbearable for a woman whose husband was overseas. One could rarely forget and there must have been a daily expectancy of bad news, briefly assuaged after the postman had called or indeed if he had not called: 'No news is good news'. Worse the heart-stopping sight of the telegraph boy praying that he was headed elsewhere. Add to this the aforementioned pressures of coping in a country at war. With the man of the house away all decision making fell to the wife (apart from those living with strong-minded parents or in-laws). It was her decision to either keep the children with her or send them away and take a job herself. War work, especially the arms production line, was the most profitable – £3 weekly, which was perhaps two thirds of a man's wage, sometimes as little as a half – but the hours were long, with twelve-hour shifts being the norm. Probably the most flexible were cleaning jobs and hairdressing work as it could be done from home. One fiercely independent widow with three children held down three cleaning jobs at the same time, working in a school, an office and a private house. Mothers with school-age children frequently worked as school dinner ladies as the hours were compatible. Many men of this generation did not approve of their wives working outside the home and few women stayed in work once they were married. Generally speaking as long as the full service allowances were coming in, finances were manageable.

But for our sample the telegram boy did arrive and the world changed. Sometimes it was not even a telegram; for Mrs Ruby Coleman it was a letter from Commodore Portsmouth dated 27 December 1940 reporting her Navy signalman husband missing and requesting her to keep the information confidential. Not until 24 May 1941 was he 'presumed to have died'. There followed weeks, months and sometimes years of appalling uncertainty and short-term allowances decreasing in value until death was confirmed or assumed. The worst communication, or lack of it, was concerning men missing in the Far East. Since the Japanese did not adhere to the Geneva Convention it might take months or even years before it was known if a man was alive or dead. The government did issue a leaflet regarding its procedures in the case of a missing man. It included the words: 'Even if no news is received that a missing man is a prisoner of war, endeavors to trace him do not cease. Enquiries are pursued not only among those who were serving with him, but also through diplomatic channels and the International Red Cross Committee at Geneva.' Perhaps some small consolation for the family.

Private Samuel Carey of the 51st Highland Division, which fought the rearguard action at St-Valery-en-Caux covering the retreat from Dunkirk, was reported missing in action on 28 June 1940 but his death was not confirmed until May 1941. The first official notification that Audrey Eastland's mother got that her husband was missing was on 5 August 1940, unofficially her husband's company sergeant major had written her a letter on 29 July. In fact her husband had been killed on 1 June while being evacuated from Dunkirk; he had managed to board a ship that was then sunk by German aircraft. It was not until 1997 that Carol Woodward actually learnt the details of the death of her merchant seaman father from enquiries instigated by her MP.

One widow remembered that the telegram announcing that her husband was missing was delivered by a young lad when she was alone in the house. No one checked up on her – there was no counselling in 1943. In Germany during the Russian campaign an American correspondent noted that the first a woman often knew of her husband's death was when her letters to him were returned, marked 'Fallen' in red ink. Ann Linford discovered only recently that her mother first learnt of the death of her husband from the wife of a fellow soldier: 'She then had to wait for the much feared telegram as confirmation.' The widow of a regular soldier in the Grenadier Guards killed at Dunkirk was on holiday in Christchurch when the telegram arrived. She, with her two small children then had a heartbreaking journey back to London, sharing the train with those soldiers fortunate enough to have survived the Dunkirk fiasco. Betty Tebbs' first husband Ernest had gone over to France on D-Day; some three months later the letters stopped coming and instead, after a two-week lull, there was an envelope marked OHMS:

> Scanning the sheet of printed paper I saw nothing except a space in the middle of the paper in which had been typed 'Killed in Action'... I ran all the way to Ernest's father's house to tell him and his two sisters the tragic news. I do not remember that 10 minute journey, I only know I could hardly speak when I got there. Pat [her daughter] not understanding what was happening but knowing that we were all upset, became distressed and I believe that it was having her and knowing that I was solely responsible for her that helped me through those terrible weeks ahead.

The following accounts from the archive detail in retrospect some of the emotional traumas of the days, weeks and years following the announcement of a serviceman's death:

> My husband was a fighter pilot No 3 Squadron. They were sent to France on May 10th when Belgium fell. He was killed three days later. He is buried in the War Cemetery at Armentieres, and it took me

eleven years before I could bear the pilgrimage to his grave. How terrible is war. We all know that and [as] I stood there amongst all the hundreds of graves from the First World War that stretched around me like a white sea, I could only think, with such clarity, of the thousands of lives that had been affected – from this one cemetery alone...

I was left at 34 in 1942 with a pension of £45 p.a. not sufficient to cover my house rent of £55. I received no advice about charitable help from the Admiralty or any other source and in my ignorance struggled for years to make ends meet. After the Admiralty telegram, the only help I received was a photograph of my husband's grave in Africa, and a pathetic sum covering the proceedings of the Sale of his few possessions'.

Under the pressure of bringing up my two sons my health has suffered, I have attempted suicide and have had psychiatric treatment. I am a Registered Disabled Person and am receiving an extra 30p a week Invalidity Benefit. But I shall have my 60th birthday in July and from then on I shall be somewhere about £2 a week worse off... I am 'Not to be subjected to strain or stress' according to the psychiatrist, when I receive my tax demand I should think I will be both strained and stressed.

Roy Pickard has done a great deal of research into the naval career of his father Harold who had joined the Royal Navy in 1923. Having already lost several ships under him in wartime service, Assistant Petty Officer Pickard was aboard HMS *Prince of Wales* when she was sunk off Malaya in December 1941. Picked up and taken to Singapore he was crewing an evacuation ship in February 1942 when that too was sunk. After an amazing tale of rescue and further escapes he was taken prisoner on Sumatra a month later. He survived more than two years' slave labour as a prisoner of war only to be tragically drowned when being shipped to mainland Japan aboard the *Harukiku Maru*. The ship was torpedoed in June 1944 by the submarine HMS *Truculent* whose officers were unaware that she was carrying Allied prisoners of war since she did not display the Red Cross. It was not until August 1946 that Harold Pickard's wife was officially informed of his death, until then he had simply been listed as 'missing'. In 1953 Mrs Pickard received a letter from a Dutch Naval officer who had been in the same camp and was able to supply some detail of her husband's time there. It would appear that for four long years she did not know if her husband was dead or alive, as the Japanese only sporadically allowed mail out of the camps.

Iris Strange had a similar sad experience, having no news of her husband following the fall of Singapore until after the war's end when one of his friends had returned home. In a letter to a *Sunday Express* writer with whom she had been in correspondence she tells the story:

> This friend was able to tell me that my husband had survived the horrors of the 'Railway' and had returned to Changi Camp. He left there again at a later date with a convoy of three boats and I gave this information to the War Office, who confirmed that this was the convoy about which there had been news when it was fired on by American submarines. Two of the boats were sunk and there were many survivors... I had heard this list read out on the radio and it was published in the newspapers, with many names known to me who had been men [serving] with my husband. His name was not among them and the War Office informed me that they believed him to be on the third boat of which there was no news. Some fifteen months after the end of the war in the Far East a communal grave was discovered on the tiny island of Balali and, while individual identification could not be made I was told that it was possible that my husband's body was one of those found...

Mrs Strange had to accept that it was highly probable that she would never really know. The prisoners on the island had been murdered and buried by their Japanese captors when the end of the war was in sight in an effort to conceal atrocities.

Men lost at sea were customarily initially posted as missing; there was no other option. Mrs Ellen Taylor was informed that her husband was reported 'missing presumed killed' on 23 September 1943 but the official notification dated 30 September states: 'There can, I fear, be no hope that your husband is still alive.' She was at least spared the long agony of hoping in vain. David Emery's father was a gunner aboard HMS *Acasta* when she was sunk along with HMS *Glorious* and HMS *Ardent* off Narvik on 8 June 1940. Over 1,500 men were lost from the three ships, some forty-six survived; only one man survived from HMS *Acasta*. In January 1941 the Admiralty were still holding out hope that Able Seaman Leonard Emery could be a prisoner of war, but it was not until October 1941 that he was presumed to have died. David Woodcock's father, who had served in the Royal Navy since 1918 and was Master at Arms aboard HMS *Glorious* was also presumed to be 'missing' on that dreadful day. Like so many other relatives of the men aboard those three ships his family waited months, even years, for some confirmation that John Frederick Woodcock might have survived and was a prisoner of war. Not until 17 March 1942 was he officially declared deceased for pension purposes but his wife Winifred never accepted the fact. As with so many women of her generation a second marriage was inconceivable – her husband had been the love of her life.

Felicity Goodall has scoured the very extensive unpublished wartime diaries, letters, etc held at the Imperial War Museum. She quotes the correspondence of Mary Brookes, the young bride of a merchant seaman who was reported missing in November 1940 when his ship the *Beaverford* was sunk. In March the following year she was informed that her husband was 'supposed' to have died. She writes: 'The word *supposed* sustained my hopes, for never at any time had I been informed that, quite categorically, all the crew had perished.'

Like so many others Mary kept hoping that her husband was somehow alive. She only accepted the fact of his death when it was confirmed by an eyewitness account in 1944.

When a ship goes down with all hands the chances of survival are slim, but when an airman is shot down or bales out over enemy territory there is always a glimmer of hope. He may have been spirited away by the Resistance – and indeed many were, especially in Holland – or be 'on the run' and later taken prisoner. A wife will keep hoping until she must accept the inevitable when it is confirmed by a third party as in the example above or when she received official notification.

Mrs Sonday's father, in the Royal Air Force Volunteer Reserve (RAFVR) and sent to the Far East, was another of those men missing 'presumed killed' in 1942. Her mother appears to have received something in order of Public Assistance for which she was means tested rather than a war widows' pension:

> Mum did various jobs during the hours we were at school to supplement her money. One job she had was at a garage at 6d per hour. It was only in later years I realised she often went without, we always had plenty of love. We had highly polished shoes very often with holes worn in the bottom, cardboard soles cut out and put inside... Mum was given a damaged parachute (nylon), it yielded material for blouses, underskirts etc... Our shopping was different. Woolworths on Saturday afternoons 6d for a bag full of broken biscuits. If the manager was not about the ladies would break some if there no broken ones left. The local greengrocer would sell you a bag of speckled fruit or veg – all the bruises cut out – for a 1d. Everybody was the same so there was a lot of help and sharing... nothing was wasted.

Which was worse, not to know if your husband was dead or alive or to be forced to watch him die?

> In 1940 my husband came home to die. We hadn't been married long. He was in the Grenadier Guards and was badly wounded in the shoulder and the spine. I watched him die over a period of four months and it was terrible. After it was over I just went to pieces, I was only 19. Eventually I pulled myself together and joined the Services where I stayed for the next four and a half years.

Some women could never accept the fact that their husband was dead, never gave up hope and remained alone for the rest of their lives. Sadly perhaps for some of these women it was discovered after the war that large numbers of deserters were adrift on the continent of Europe; even in 1943 it was estimated that some 16,000 servicemen were Absent Without Leave (AWOL) in the British Isles. At least the women who had received confirmation of their husbands' deaths knew the worst and must face the future as a widow. How must they have felt when the war ended and other men came home to their wives is unimaginable: their loneliness must have been appalling. That these homecomings were often idealised did not diminish the anguish of the widows, although they at least did not have to cope with the undoubted traumas of men trying to adjust to civilian life.

Widowhood is agonising for any woman; some deal with it by retreating into the shell of the home they shared with their husbands, others find solace with women in the same situation. Sometimes they join a group with whom they can share experiences or perhaps – these days – have counselling. Others refuse to be labelled 'widow' and wouldn't dream of joining or associating themselves with any organisation which would remind them of the fact. Any married woman of advancing years has at the back of her mind a premonition of widowhood. It is in the nature of things. The organisation CRUSE (named for the biblical widow's cruse which never ran out of oil) set up in 1959 to provide support and counselling for widows, was also '... committed to breaking the stigma around grief...' They acknowledge the differences between the classic perception of a widow and that of the younger service wife. There is currently a training course specifically aimed at counselling the service widow and her children, which recognises that the death of a husband is harder to face when the man is in the prime of life and the children are still young. For the widows of career servicemen there is a triple bereavement as they lose husband, home and social structure in one operation.

In many societies the widow is ostracised by custom or religion. Most do not go quite as far as 'suttee' where a Hindu widow would throw herself onto her husband's funeral pyre thereby solving her own and everyone else's embarrassment. The widow in her son's house must in many cultures take second place to the daughter-in-law, while the English aristocracy traditionally banished her to the 'Dower House', her status diminished. In Victorian England any widow who could afford it had to dress entirely in black for the first year at least, and was therefore immediately recognisable. In Mediterranean countries it is, or was, the same, though the widow's status may be different. At dinner parties hostesses usually favoured the single man in preference to the widowed woman. The invisibility of the lone elderly woman in a restaurant is marked when she is ushered to the worst table and the bad service that goes with it. Social mores have changed dramatically in the last thirty years but for the young widows of the Second World War it was the post-war era that was the most significant. Even today in a more loose-knit society the widow is an anachronism. She doesn't want to seem to be too dependent so perhaps makes an appearance of being independent and keeping her misery to herself. She has often lost her social status and is far too frequently rejected by her married friends who see her as a threat. It is just as difficult for family and friends who want to help; there is no simple way or solution now and there never has been. The war widow simply has more to contend with.

Not surprisingly perhaps, only one lady respondent actually mentioned sex. This is not surprising because it would not occur to that generation to do so and nor does it pay to make assumptions. Some women – without efficient contraception – might have found the absence of a man something of a relief. Many people in the 1940s lived at very real poverty levels and in such conditions wife beating was not unusual. Even at middle-class levels marriage was not necessarily entirely blissful. In *Hidden Lives* there is a reference to contemporary play *The Years Between* where a man reported killed in action reappears, much to his wife's distress as she had thought herself rid of a domineering husband. It is also as well to remember that many marriages were contracted in wartime haste, probably not all of them to the 'right' man. Ernest Bevin, then minister for labour, estimated in November

1943 that there had been 2.25 million marriages since September 1939. Divorces also escalated at an alarming rate both during the war and in the immediate post-war period: 12,314 cited in 1944 up to 60,190 in 1947.

However we are talking about young women in their twenties or thirties, and many must have succumbed and had discreet affairs with other men, perhaps with the lodger – a feature of the 1940s and '50s when home owning was still uncommon – an employer or one from the endless supply of lonely servicemen. Sadly, whatever they did would have been subject to gossip and criticism; one widow from a small Scottish town said she always had to be very careful even about speaking to a man in the street for everything was noted and commented upon. It is significant that so many of the widows in our sample never remarried, sometimes it was because they would lose their war widows' pension but often it was simply because no one else could compare. Helen Smith's parents were married on 12 April 1941 and her father was lost on 8 May 1941 when the HMS *Ramillies* was torpedoed. It was a marriage of only three weeks but effectively for a lifetime:

> My mother did not remarry although she had several opportunities to do so. She told me that she did not consider any of them a suitable father for me but I do not think any of them measured up to her beloved husband who she missed more and more towards the end of her life despite their short time together.

> Mother considered herself to be married to Dad for all her lifetime.

> My mother always said she would never have anyone else looking after Dad's children.

> My mother could never accept that my father was dead.

Many women never did get over the emotional trauma triggered by the news of the death of their husband:

My mother never recovered from the shock of receiving the dreaded telegram and for the rest of her life suffered regular bouts of depression, no doubt made worse by the every present shortage of money.

[My mother] found life very difficult, culminating in a nervous breakdown in 1961.

He was my life, what do I do now?

I recall that during my teens I would hear her [my mother] crying at night and at times of stress, she would sometimes say 'George why did you leave me?'

Mother was on medication for psoriasis and other stress related ills.

[My mother] attempted suicide twice.

She was always depressed and poorly – when Dad died, part of her died too.

At one time I might have thought a breakdown was a sort of romantic thing to have. It isn't. It is horrible. I used to be travelling on the underground to work and tears would stream down my face... I eventually went to the doctor and she said 'You're having a breakdown dear, you'd better knock off work for a bit'. This breakdown – I suppose it went on and off for two or three years – would stop me in my tracks. I would feel as if I were going to fall over backwards. I wanted to hold onto something all the time...

(Extract from *What Did You Do In the War Mummy?*)

Some women although they did remarry perhaps for security or to provide a father figure for their child never really got over the tragedy of that first marriage: 'My mother was emotionally very fragile and very timid. I often felt I was looking after her.'

Others appeared determined to look forward rather than back. Barbara Lane's mother never again mentioned her husband. Josephine Smith's mother remarried in 1948 and 'put her first marriage out of her mind and tried very hard to turn me into a "Winter" [her stepfather's name].' Betty Tebbs married again some two years after her first husband's death and with her new husband, Len, her life took a different path. It must have required enormous strength of character not to remarry when the opportunity presented itself. One widow was tempted but refused to have the prospective mother-in-law living with them; the erstwhile bridegroom chose his mother. A surprising proportion of our correspondents just opted to remain single, always working to support their children. One determined lady who lost her husband in Hong Kong on that appalling Christmas Day in 1941, later managed to flee with her small son to Kunming then held by the Nationalist Chinese where she worked as a secretary in the British Liaison Office. Returning to Hong Kong after the war she worked all her long life to give her child the education and upbringing she felt was his due, as did countless other women:

My mother suffered no nervous illness, just 'got on with it'.

My mother was a fighter and worked very hard to give me a good and happy life... The lady my mother had worked for before her marriage visited regularly with sheets needing 'edge to middle' and collars and cuffs to be turned. There was always something for my money box...

My mother worked all her life as she never remarried ... her first job after father's death was as a core-maker in the local engineering factory working the night shift. As we got older she worked as a cook in the Newcastle Royal Victoria Infirmary, starting work at 6 am, often walking four miles to work.

[My mother] became more withdrawn and kept herself to herself. She had no friends outside the family and became very independent, never asking for help from anyone.

Thanks to my mother who loved us all and gave up her life for ours.
I would like my Mum to be recognised for the wonderful way she
coped with five children – all girls.
(Audrey Eastland)

Grandma never remarried but was reported to have been 'friendly
with the coalman'.

Probably the most fortunate – if such a term is appropriate – were
the women who had a private income, a career or had had professional training before marriage. Helen Smith's mother went back
to teaching, initially leaving Helen in the care of her grandmother.
An officer's son, Michael Bishop's school fees were paid for by the
War Office. To get away from her mother-in-law his mother took
a job as assistant matron at the same boarding school. This 'tough'
lady always worked and in 1955 was one of the first women in
the country to get a mortgage in her own name to buy a house
in Colchester. To help pay off the mortgage she took in tenants, a
pattern she was to continue for the rest of her life.

One entry quoted in *Private Battles*, a collection of Mass
Observation diary extracts edited by Simon Garfield, strikes a
rather odd note: 'Stopped on the way back from work and called
on M... L... who came swimming with me. Her husband John was
in the RAMC in Normandy, last weekend he was reported seriously
wounded, and today he was reported dead ... she is remarkably
courageous about it...' They swim together again a few days later
with no further mention of her widowhood. Felicity Goodall in
Voices From the Home Front relates a similar experience. The day she
learnt of her husband's presumed death one young woman went
straight to bed. The following day she felt she had to get out so
went to the cinema, and the day after that went back to work but
never really accepted the fact that her husband was gone until
she received a letter from an eyewitness. Many women held out
hope for years and could only accept the fact of their husband's
death when they had confirmation from another, more personal,
source. One surprising comment from a Mass Observation diarist

illustrates the other side of the coin. She determines that should her husband be listed as missing she would find another man to sleep with: 'it did not matter what man, as long as it was a man, and if her husband was killed she meant to do so immediately.'

The shock news of widowhood was often followed by the reality of homelessness, particularly in the case of those living in service housing. Literally only a few days after being notified of her husband's death at Dunkirk came the letter asking one lady to vacate their married quarters. Audrey Eastland's mother was given forty-eight hours to leave their dockland accommodation when her husband went to war. In 1942 widows were usually given six weeks' notice. This varied enormously over the years, at the time of the Falklands War in 1982, for example the RAF required widows to vacate in two months.

Finding somewhere to live at an affordable rent was near impossible for most people. During the war housing was scarce – in November 1944 it was estimated that one in three houses was damaged – and throughout the 1950s accommodation was at a premium. Another Mass Observation diarist writes in November 1944: 'Meg and Roger (newlyweds) have been frantically searching for other accommodation for weeks. The housing shortage is really scandalous.' On other occasions she records '...another letter from S... asking me to find an unfurnished house or flat in this area... He might as well ask for the moon...' and '...fantastic prices are being asked for the poorest class of dwelling...' How much worse then was it for widows on a meagre pension? Ruby Coleman, desperately trying to get a place of her own, found that landlords wanted a husband's name on the rent book. She eventually found a fire-damaged upstairs flat and refrained from telling the landlady that she was a war widow. For three rooms she paid 16s 6d a week, leaving 16s to feed and clothe herself and son. Fortunately her sister moved in to help with expenses and, as the rent was always paid on time, nothing was said. When Janet Stubbins lost her father the family immediately had to move from their rented house with all mod cons (12s 6d per week) to a tiny cottage (7s 6d per week) with one room downstairs, two small bedrooms upstairs, no kitchen, no bathroom and an outside toilet shared with neighbours.

When the War Widows' Association was in its embryonic stage a lady from Glasgow responded to the publicity trawl. Her letter itemised the difficulties that were common to so many war widows in this country over the years:

> (14 December 1971)
>
> I was widowed in 1944, and my daughter was 16 months old. Naturally I had to resume work at anything I could get. Again I had to pay the big insurance stamp, I had no choice. At the time I did not have a home of my own, and since then I have had to remain a lodger, right up to the present day. I have not a cat's chance in China of ever possessing a house of my own, rented or otherwise. Once, I was told by a woman assistant at the Council Office to come back when I had five children. What way I was to obtain this family I shall never know. Even [in] this modern day I still cannot get a book out of the Public Library as I am not a rate payer. If I [want] a book my sister has to sign the form. I have lived in this district all my life. Like many others I sometimes wonder what my husband gave his life for...

Catherine Barnett can remember moving to Stockton when her mother was widowed; Catherine was four and her sibling eleven months. They were to be more fortunate on the housing front:

> My mother worked in a factory humping sacks of paint pigment. I seem to remember she also had cleaning jobs. Apart from that we were homeless and 'lived in' with other families or elderly ladies with a spare front room and a bedroom. We ended up living in a Nissen hut in an abandoned army camp, until we were awarded a brand new house on a post war housing estate in 1952. At the age of 12 this was the first time I had lived in a house with a bathroom, indoor toilet and hot water on tap.

From the evidence it would seem that most war widows initially moved in or continued to live with relatives or tried to find

1 Maureen Shaw's parents, Martha and John Whyte, photographed early in 1940.

2 A standard army postcard sent from Durban, South Africa, en route to India.

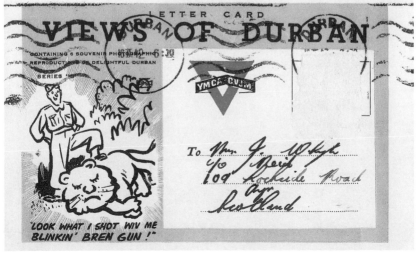

3 John Frederick Woodcock
Master-at-Arms, HMS Glorious.

4 Telegram informing the family that
John Woodcock is missing in action off
Norway, April 1940.

Charges to pay
s.   d.
RECEIVED
Central Telegraph
Office, E.C.1.

No.
OFFICE STAMP

POST OFFICE
TELEGRAM

Prefix. Time handed in. Office of Origin and Service Instructions. Words.

From   51
51   11.15 PLYMOUTH   35

To

MR WOODCOCK C/O MR S CORRY 44 BEACONSFIELD ROAD   EDMONTON
LONDON N -9

= DEEPLY REGRET TO INFORM YOU THAT YOUR BROTHER
JOHN P WOODCOCK MASTER AT ARMS D/M 39878 IS MISSING
POSSIBLY PRISONER OF WAR = COMMODORE DEVONPORT +

CT 44 9 39878 +

For free repetition of doubtful words telephone "TELEGRAMS ENQUIRY" or call, with this form
at office of delivery. Other enquiries should be accompanied by this form and, if possible, the envelope.

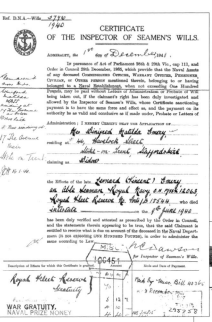

5 The official certificate which will permit Winifred Emery to claim her late husband's effects (as long as their value did not exceed £100).

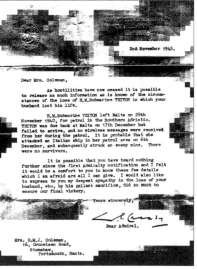

6 After five long years Mrs Coleman is finally notified by the Admiralty in November 1945 as much as is known of the circumstances of her husband's death in the submarine HMS Triton, which disappeared in late 1940.

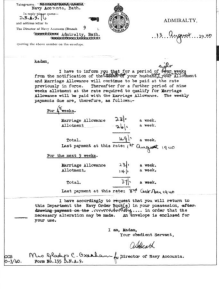

7 Admiralty notification of the allowances Mrs Gladys Oxenham would receive during the period that her husband is officially posted missing in action.

Hawks Grove
Beddingham
Sx.
19/3/42

Dear Mrs Pickard
I am writing to give you some news of your husband. He is almost certainly a prisoner of war in Sumatra.
All naval personnel were evacuated from Singapore on the night of 12th Feb, making for Batavia. I was detailed for an old steamer called 'King Lud' — was Pickard.
We were sunk by bombs the next morning, but got ashore to an uninhabited island where we spent for a week before getting by Junk to Sumatra. We (a party of 50) crossed Sumatra mostly by river to Padang on the W. coast, where the Navy from Colombo had been taking people off. When we arrived on March 6th there was about 600 service men from Singapore with about 8th the Dutch E.I. fell to the Japs

who were only about 150 miles away and as no more ships were going to come from Colombo, it was evident we should all be made prisoners. Being all survivors we had very little arms or gear. I was ordered with other officers by the Colonel in charge to make a break for Colombo (1600 miles) in a Malay dhow which he had procured, so as to be of further use in the war. Thus at the time appeared to have small chance, but we were picked up off Ceylon after 27 days. Pickard was — Lest saw him. We were both together in P. of W. and used to talk talk a lot about revolver shooting. He was also under me in a Guard Job at the Singapore depot and so I got to know him well. Hoping you will get him back safe and sound as soon as possible.

Yours sincerely
G.A.G. Brooke
Lieut. R.N.

HMS Prince of Wales

8 Letter to Mrs Harold Pickard from a former shipmate of her husband, who was with him when their ship was sunk on 12 February 1942, whilst fleeing the Japanese en route from Singapore to Batavia.

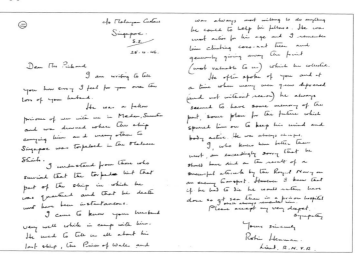

c/o Malayan Customs
Singapore.
S.S.
25.4.46.

Dear Mrs Pickard
I am writing to tell you how sorry I feel for you over the loss of your husband.
He was a fellow prisoner of war with me in Medan, Sumatra and was downed when the ship carrying him and many others to Singapore was torpedoed in the Malacca Straits.
I understand from those who survived that the torpedo hit that part of the ship in which he was quartered and that his death must have been instantaneous.
I came to know your husband very well while in camp with him. He used to tell us all about his last ship, the Prince of Wales and

was always most willing to do anything he could to help his fellows. He was most active for his age and I remember him climbing coco-nut trees and generally giving away the fruit (most valuable to us) which he collected.
He often spoke of you and at a time when many men grew depressed (and not without reason) he always seemed to have some memory of the past, some plan for the future which spurred him on to keep his mind and body active. He was always cheerful.
I, who knew him better than most, am exceedingly sorry that he should have died as the result of a successful attack by the Royal Navy on an enemy transport. However I know that if he had to die he would rather have done so at sea than in a prison hospital, as I such always reminded him.
Please accept my very deepest sympathy.

Yours sincerely
Robin Henman.
Lieut. R.N.V.R.

9 Not until 1946 does Mrs Pickard find out the circumstances of her husband's death from a fellow POW who was with him when the Japanese ship which was carrying them back to Singapore across the Medan Strait was ironically and tragically struck by a torpedo from a Royal Navy submarine.

Opposite top, left to right
10 Certificate, formally confirming that Harold Pickard had died, this was not issued until 1 December 1945.

11 Not until 1997, after she had pursued the matter through her local MP, did Carol Woodward discover the detail's of her father's death.

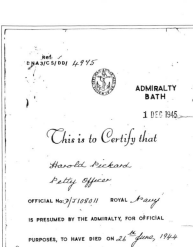

MINISTRY OF DEFENCE
MAIN BUILDING WHITEHALL LONDON SW1A 2HB
Telephone 0171-21.................(Direct Dialling)
0171-21 89600 (Switchboard)

PARLIAMENTARY UNDER-SECRETARY OF STATE
FOR DEFENCE

D/US of S/JS 4263/97/M   November 1997

Dear Paddy,

Thank you for your letter of 27 October to George Robertson enclosing one from your constituent, Mrs C A Woodward of 131 Barbara Square, Hucknall, about the loss of the ZURICHMOOR. I am replying as this matter falls within my area of responsibility.

The 4,455 gross registered tonnage Moor Line steamer SS ZURICHMOOR left Halifax, Nova Scotia, on 21 May 1942 in ballast for St Thomas in the Virgin Islands, where she was due on 31 May but failed to arrive. Nothing was subsequently heard from her and she and her crew of 39 plus six gunners were presumed lost. It was later deduced from a German radio broadcast that she had probably been the victim of a U-boat on 24 May when some 200 miles south of Cape Sable, but it was not until the end of the war, when the German naval records were seized by the Allies, that her actual fate could be established.

The ZURICHMOOR was sunk at 1825 local time (2225 GMT) on 22 May 1942 in position 40°46'N,64°54'W, which is approximately 300 miles east of Long Island, by the German U-boat U 432 under the command of Kapitänleutnant Heinz Otto Schultze. Schultze had first sighted the ZURICHMOOR two hours earlier and five minutes later had dived for a submerged attack. He fired two torpedoes, one of which struck the ship forward and the other aft, and she went down by the head within a minute and a half. U 432 thereupon surfaced, and inspecting the wreckage Schultze came upon a nameplate bearing the name ZURICHMOOR. Schultze makes no mention of having seen survivors and, in view of the rapidity with which the ship sank, the whole crew are believed to have gone down with her.

I hope this information will help to set Mrs Woodward's mother's mind at rest.

JOHN SPELLAR MP

Left 12 Three-year-old Bryan Bliss in Kunming, China where he spent the rest of war after escaping from Hong Kong with his mother.

Below 13 The Kirkee Commonwealth War Graves Cemetery at Pune (Poona), India where Sergeant Whyte is buried.

14 Bernard and Joan Bishop, photograph taken in 1939 or 1940.

15 Michael Bishop was born in 1941. His father, Bernard, by then promoted to captain, was killed when his Bren Gun Carrier overturned during training in Scotland for D-Day.

16 King George VI together with Queen Elizabeth meeting widows and children of members of the crew of the Ajax and the Exeter, ships which sustained heavy losses and casualties during the Battle of the River Plate, the first major naval battle of the Second World War in December 1939. Winston Churchill is present in the foreground.

17 Ernest and Elizabeth (Betty) Whewell with baby Patricia, taken when Ernest was on leave.

Below 18 Betty Tebbs representing the British branch of the National Women's Association at the International Women's Assembly against nuclear testing, held in Moscow at the Lenin Stadium in 1986. Valentina Tereshcova, the first spacewoman, is on the left of the picture; Betty is third from left.

19 Iris Strange, President and Secretary of the British War Widows and Associates, displaying the petitions for equal pensions for all war widows in 1984.

20 Iris Strange (far left) and members of the British War Widows and Associates celebrating achieving parity of pensions for all war widows.

lodgings at a price they could afford. One widow rooming in a house in Middlesex with her small son made sweets to sell, her only way to make some extra cash. Another, widowed in 1941, had to spend three years in a rest centre before she got a one-bedroom flat. Sadly as mentioned earlier there are quite a few examples of widows having no option but to put their children into temp-orary or permanent care until accommodation became available:

> I had no capital and my boy went at 8 years into a home, as I had no home and had to take domestic work to get a roof over my head … the Council would not give accommodation as I did not have enough income.

Officers' widows too had problems finding somewhere to live. This advertisement appeared in the personal column of *The Times* in October 1946:

> Widow of Regular Army officer 38 desires any reasonable OCCUPATION; accommodation desirable; has own furniture; child home on holidays; untrained but cheerful and adaptable and willing to learn. Offers welcomed.

This was mirrored by Ena Mitchell who put an advertisement in the local paper for a room in a house for which she would pay rent and do housework. There had been an article in the *Sunday Graphic* commenting on the shortage of domestic servants. However, noted the writer, there were always war widows whose only hope was a 'live-in' job where they could keep a child: 'They will accept a £1 a week, run a house single-handed or look after your children … there are more of these women than there are jobs for them...'

When Elizabeth Robert's husband was killed in 1944 she was living with her mother-in-law who almost immediately told her to find somewhere else to live. Elizabeth, with two young chil-dren, ended up in one room, her furniture consisting of a bed and a cot. It was only due to a one-off payment of £48 from the army that she was able to buy the necessities. Probably the majority did live with relatives; many servicemen's wives would automatically move back to the maternal home when their husbands were posted:

> My mother was already living with her parents when my father was killed because they had not been married long.

> I was living with my parents at the time my husband was killed. Continued living with them until getting remarried.

> …[we] were staying with them [my grandparents] when Dad was killed. We continued to stay there for several months until after my younger brother was born.

> …we subsequently moved to live with grandparents.

The latter remark occurs frequently. Without family support with accommodation, financial handouts, help with child care and providing holidays many widows would not have been able to cope at all. Audrey Eastland's mother with her five daughters had no option but to move in with her own mother who still had other family living with her. Four adults and five children all lived in a two-bedroom cottage.

> My mother had no alternative but to go home. Soldier's wives received £5 to move, they took all the places for rent, nothing for us.

> Mum didn't work, I think my maternal grandparents and aunt were very good to us.

Betty Tebbs was fortunate to have been renting a house of her own when her husband Ernest was killed. Her mother, she says, gave her a very sound piece of advice, suggesting that she live with them for three months and then decide whether or not to return to her own home. She stayed with her parents for a mere two weeks; that was enough. She had been independent too long to want to return to even a whisper of parental control.

Another respondent recalls her mother saying that she regretted for the rest of her life moving back to the family home when her husband was posted abroad. It was what was expected, it being improper for a young woman to live on her own. It was also expected, when she was widowed, that she would have sole responsibility for taking care of her own aged mother, the logic being that her four sisters had their own husbands to look after. Chris Beatty's response to our request for information succinctly sums up all these aspects:

> My father was killed in action in France on 22nd July 1944, he was 29, I was 3 years old. My mother never recovered from the shock of receiving the dreaded telegram and for the rest of her life suffered regular bouts of depression, no doubt made worse by the ever present shortage of money. Each year she would get an increase in her war widow's pension (pittance she always called it) and there would be an almost similar increase in the Council rent. She would say they give with one hand and take with the other.

For women whose husbands are lost on a 'far distant shore' there is often a great longing so see where he is buried for themselves and to pay a final farewell. This became a real issue after 1982 when the women widowed by the Falklands conflict were given free travel to visit their husbands' graves. Clement Freud MP asked of the Prime Minister on Monday 18 July 1983: 'if she will estimate in each case the number of widows whose husbands are buried abroad; and if she will ensure that funds are made available, to those widows who wish to do so, to visit their husbands' graves...'

The Prime Minister's reply went as follows:

> Since 1967 the next of kin of a serviceman buried overseas has been permitted either a visit to attend the funeral, or if this is not possible

a subsequent visit within the next two years to see the grave, at public expense, together with a companion. The Government decided at the time that this concession could not be granted retrospectively, and this remains the case...

It is not surprising then that a lot of newspaper coverage was given to Mrs Noreen Battams, whose husband had been killed in 1941 and was buried in the Ismalia War Cemetery alongside the Suez Canal. Mrs Battams said that she had written to the Ministry of Defence in 1962 asking for financial help to visit the cemetery. She was told she would have to go at her own expense and received the same reply when she asked again after 1982. Her local MP then contacted her to say that the government had given the RBL a grant to help widows in these circumstances. 'I put my name down to go' said Mrs Battams '... but then I received a letter from the War Widows' Association. They said the British Legion still expect us to finance ourselves.'

This was yet another bone of contention for Iris Strange. The government refusal to grant free travel for the widows of earlier conflicts can be understood to some degree. A member of the House of Lords stated that help was out of the question because of the sheer numbers involved – he quoted 172,000. 'Rubbish' was Iris' reaction; she had been unable to find a single First World War widow fit enough to undertake any journey and estimated that something in the region of 50,000 would be the more accurate figure. She went on to say: 'Thousands of us, and I am one, have no idea where our husbands are buried, or even what became of them, so we can be counted out.' The general furore over this apparently did make some difference because a year or so later the government paid for 230 widows to visit their husbands' graves in the Far East following complaints that the 'Forgotten Army' had been forgotten again.

There was also an emotional need for simple recognition. Preparations to commemorate the fortieth anniversary of the Normandy landings – D-Day – failed to include either any widow or any official representation from any war widows' association.

An article in the *Sunday Mirror* dated 27 May 1984 quotes one widow: 'I think that at least some of us who lost their men in Normandy should have pride of place in the D-Day ceremonies on June 6. Surely the women who lost their men have a right to be there.' No doubt prodded by the negative publicity, the Ministry of Defence did a quick *volte-face* and invited fifty widows – the first fifty who telephoned a special number – to the commemoration with the following provisos: they must be fit to travel and their husbands had to have been killed on 6 June. The same can be said of the annual Service of Remembrance held at the Cenotaph. Where were the widows? For many years the WWA organised their own ceremony the day before, laying their own crosses and wreaths. Simply further examples of the ways in which for many years after the Second World War the women widowed by that conflict were sidelined and excluded from ceremonies that might have given them some small comfort.

Six

WAR ORPHANS

THE MAJORITY of British servicemen in the Second World War, as in the First World War, were not regulars but conscripts. They recognised that they were fighting for Britain's survival. The widows many of them were to leave behind were also fighting for survival, particularly for the survival and welfare of their children. One such was Kay Davey, whose husband was to die from tuberculosis contracted when liberating the Belsen concentration camp:

My first concern was always for my daughter's care and upbringing.

This was the maxim that guided widows' lives in their struggle to bring up their families during the war and in the years of austerity that followed. That the children did appreciate all the sacrifices made by their mothers is evident in the letters received from their progeny:

We never had much but she always made sure we had food. It was only in later years I realised how often she went without.

It is only when one gets older does one realise the sacrifices mother must have made to keep the family clothed and fed. I often wonder how my life may have changed had my father survived the war.

My mother had a thyroid problem but postponed an operation until she was sure I could look after myself whilst she was in hospital.

No holidays, very little meat, mostly vegetables but through it all we came out the other end, thanks to my mother who loved us all and gave up her life for ours.

My mother brought 3 of us up very strictly – 2 sets of clothes. Life was very bleak but we didn't know any different. One apple at Christmas, I remember it was a red one.

The following letter from David Blackburn well illustrates the anger that these children felt at the cavalier treatment meted out to their widowed mothers by successive governments:

As an only child born before 1939 to a war casualty, here are a few pointers. As a widow in 1945 you have lost, you are an embarrassment, just another casualty to be ignored, if possible, which is why you can find very little on the subject. From married quarters in 1942 you were evicted within 6 weeks (now 6 months). You are alone in a man's world, competing for a man's job but paid pin money wages if successful. You will have difficulty in obtaining a loan or a mortgage, if you buy a house you pay extra tax under schedule A, if you are lucky enough to receive a war widow's pension it is taxed as 'unearned income'. To add insult to injury, having sacrificed your husband and the father of your children, you will not be welcome at the Cenotaph on Remembrance Day, only allowed to be there when you creep past when no-one is looking. Don't rain on my parade? There is no man to look after the finances, do the garden, be the handyman, advise and guide the children, be a role model, it's all down to you [the widow] in what was, in 1940s Britain, a real man's world. Shall I go on, or does that give you enough flavour?

In 2008 David published a book of poems, with the proceeds going to Water Aid. In it was the following, titled 'Conviction':

> It's fine for MPs to have convictions
> It's the war widows who face eviction.
> And what of a sad child, left all alone
> Who is now in a 'single parent' home?
> So no more children, husband, father, dead
> One soldier died, now see the ripples spread,
> So when, on their 'convictions' MPs act
> One questions, how many will think of that?

His childhood experiences obviously made a deep and lasting impression.

A letter written to Iris Strange in the 1980s is of the same ilk: this man never forgot or forgave the country which allowed his mother to starve after her husband was killed in the First World War; he attached her menu for one week which we have reproduced in full:

> 1 small wholemeal loaf
> 4oz butter
> 4oz tea
> 6 1d Oxo cubes
> 3d worth fish bits for Sunday dinner
> 6d bag broken biscuits
> ½ pint milk a day
> 2oz jar of jam a week – and so to bed cold and hungry....
> No firing, only sticks from hedging and bits of cardboard
> 1d candle to sew on a patch, darn a sock and warm the air in the room

Apparently this lady literally starved to death and what so enraged her son was the newspaper headline of the time: 'Wycombe Woman Starves Herself to Death' as though it were self-inflicted.

In 1944 Sir Ian Fraser's motion that: 'Neither a widow or a child should be financially penalised by the death or disablement of a husband or father on service' was backed by many MPs but not by government action. During, and in the years immediately after the war, most people in Britain lived from week to week ('everything was managed weekly') and often in difficult living conditions. As things gradually improved in the late 1950s and '60s so too did the general standard of living – for example many families now possessed a washing machine – but not for war widows and their children.

> Other children's fathers came home and they began to prosper while we remained the same...Things didn't improve much until my sister started work. Then she had electricity put in and other improvements made. However my mother never had an easy life. She was in and out of hospital for years, leaving us in the care of relatives. When my sister was 14 and I was 10 we rebelled and said we would stay home on our own...
> (Margaret Hothi)

Arthur Marwick, writing in the 1980s, observed that while the 1940s are only forty years ago they are 'light years compared to the lives of people today'. A war widow then, in effect had to sacrifice her own needs to those of her children in ways that are not often seen today. She would rarely have any social life; it was difficult to pursue any kind of social activity when every penny had to be used for essentials. Many widows were bitter at being left behind in the country's growing prosperity. In France the children of war dead were known as 'The Children of the Nation'. In Britain no such high-sounding phrase was ever coined; in official documents they were simply referred to as 'war orphans'. The perception remained among war widows and their children that the government in power – whichever party – had no interest in them and the financial hardships they had to bear. Any small increase in the pension was usually matched by a corresponding increase in rent or utility bills. Most women tried to shield their children from the worst aspects of poverty, often at risk to their own health. Many paid for the children's school meals to spare them the embarrassment of standing up in the classroom every Monday morning and publicly confessing to receiving free school meals, which was the usual procedure at the time. Rather tactlessly perhaps, a nursery teacher announced to the entire class that one little girl did not have a daddy, something the rest of the children found difficult to believe. Everybody had a father in the days of the standard family unit, did they not?

Individual acts of kindness were remembered with gratitude. As mentioned earlier, Janet Stubbins was 'adopted' by the American Red Cross at the instigation of the British Legion. She received much needed financial support and gifts at a time when her mother was fighting for a War Widow's Pension. Hilary Hare had an American foster parent who sent regular monthly donations and gifts of clothing at Christmas. Hilary kept in touch with her benefactor until the latter's death. Daphne Hartley's mother saved any birthday and Christmas gifts of money from friends at church to buy her shoes.

Isolated examples of philanthropy, however gratefully received, did not compensate for the lack of interest and adequate financial support from the government of the day. War widows and their children justifiably felt that the government, and indeed the nation, had little interest in them or their straitened circumstances. Providing for the family was a constant anxiety; the widows had to balance being at home for their children with the necessity of working to supplement the pension. Childcare facilities were almost non-existent immediately after the war, most women had to rely on family for practical and financial support. For children fortunate enough to be surrounded by grandparents, aunts, uncles and cousins, life was more secure and the mother was then often able to go out to work.

> I cannot stress enough the support from both sides of the family – to my mother and to me.
> (Foster Watson)

> I never felt the lack of a father figure since I was surrounded by numerous aunts, cousins and grandparents who loved, cherished and spoilt me.

A war widow without family back up was faced with an insolvable dilemma. She could work part-time as a school dinner lady for example – and many did – a job that was very poorly paid but had the huge advantage that she would be at home when her children came home from school. But if no part-time work was available she either had to stay at home and manage on the meagre pension or work longer hours that did not fit in with the children's schedule. Every war widow's focus was on keeping the family together: what else did she have? For many, in the aftermath of bereavement, the children were a reason to carry on. Sadly some were not able to keep their children with them. A combination of circumstances – inadequate housing, illness, inability to work, lack of child care or family support – meant that in spite of all the mother's efforts, some children had to go into a children's home. In March 1945 the NSPCC recommended that widows rather than spinsters should be put in charge of such homes. It was always hoped that this would be a temporary measure but inevitably this was not always the case and some children did permanently end up in orphanages. The anguish this would cause to mother and child is almost unimaginable: the mother's feeling of loss and guilt and the sense of desertion and desolation felt by the children. Orphanages in those years could still be Dickensian; much depended on the personality of the woman in charge, which was very much the luck of the draw. The following letter, written by Iris Strange who had little choice but to put her son into an orphanage, is self-explanatory:

There were few facilities for working mothers to have their children cared for and those who had no supporting family help fared very badly; our take home pay was so small that we could not afford to make realistic payments to neighbours and friends to look after our children. In my own case I had no help from my family and, because I could not afford to pay anyone to look after my small son, Tony became more and more rebellious because he had to come home to an empty house. As he grew older he naturally became more adventurous and he took to escaping from school after I had taken him there on my way to work; and many times he was not only missing when I arrived home but he was missing all night too. Eventually the long summer holidays

brought the crisis and I had to obtain help to put him into an orphanage. It broke my heart – and his. He had already lost his beloved father
and he then thought he had lost me and his home. I shall never forgive
those uncaring governments who deliberately added the misery of
poverty to our bereavement and brought Tony and me, and many other
war widows and their children, to this heart-rending situation.

Tony, aged eleven, was put into a National Children's Home at
Harpenden. Iris adds: 'I used to visit him there about once a
month and our relationship became strained because he thought
I had ditched him.' It is impossible not to be moved by this grief-
stricken letter and not to feel anger that mothers were driven to
such measures. Iris Strange and others like her put their children
into orphanages to keep them safe, unaware of a government
scheme in place to send some of these children to Australia
without the knowledge or consent of their parents. We do not
know for certain how many of these child emigrants were the
children of war widows but, in the light of the recent revela-
tions on this shameful episode it is quite likely that some of them
were included in the scheme. Janis Lomas discovered an item in
the national press in 1947, issued apparently by the Ministry of
Pensions, appealing for foster homes for war orphans: '100 baby
boys – what offers? You can take a baby on trial.'

For boys the absence of a male role model could be an added
problem:

The absence of a male role model (or surrogate father figure) as I was
growing up was something that I felt quite deeply. I learned that my
father had many attributes and I felt, as a child and as a teenager, that I
was quite unable to measure up...
(Foster Watson)

In those days a working mother was frowned upon and boys brought
up without a father were expected to be always in trouble.

Not always however, David Blackburn writes:

In order to make sure I didn't become a latch key kid the pair of them [his mother and aunt who lived with them] went into service as cook/ housekeeper and lady's maid from 1947 until 1956... I never considered I was deprived at any time through lack of a father... I had a very happy childhood thanks to my mother and aunt, but they were the ones who had to struggle, it was never me who felt any loss or pressure. After all, as a child, you only know what you are used to...

Where possible, a boarding school education often ensured that a boy had male mentors and companionship. Officers' widows could have their children educated at boarding school at government expense instead of receiving child allowance; sometimes the wealthier members of the family would help with school fees. Some children would benefit from the experience; a seven-year-old boy sent from Hong Kong to prep school in England did not feel the lack of a father because all the children were in the same situation: no parents were in evidence and the atmosphere at school was a happy one. Others have bad memories. Bob Grainger remembers being sent to a boarding school in Surrey where life was harsh and there was a lot of bullying. One day the art teacher made the children run round the school playing field until they collapsed – one child only had one lung – and it was only brought to a halt when the school nurse intervened. This punishment was for yawning!

Many fatherless boys passed through the childhood and teenage years in the shadow of a father they had never known or could barely remember but who was always held up to them as the apotheosis of manhood. This acted as a spur to some boys, driving them on to do well, while others reacted by feeling unable to 'measure up' and only realising their full potential in adulthood. Some boys became rebellious; one boy very much resented being corrected by his uncles and sundry male lodgers and reacted with: 'You are not my father.' However there were some happier memories. One widow's son was the only boy in his school to have lost his father. The fathers of his friends would include him in their outings such as going to football matches: 'Probably they had all lost friends during the war and it was their way of being glad they had survived.'

Many war widows for whom a career would have been unimportant or unobtainable determined that their children should have a career of their choice 'something to fall back on should the need arise' as Sheila Cameron's mother told her daughter. Sheila was to become a primary school teacher, a not uncommon choice among the children of war widows. The 1944 Education Act established secondary education for every child stipulating that no local Education Authority would henceforth be permitted to charge fees. It did however reinforce the two-tier system already in place; the fortunate minority who passed the Eleven-Plus examination went on to grammar school. Many of our respondents recall this watershed in their lives, not always happily. One widow was fortunate enough to receive 10s a week for the period of one year when her daughter passed the exam. But to get the money she had to visit the house of someone 'in high places' while the daughter waited outside, since she – the recipient – was not allowed into the house!

It was for some not an enjoyable experience, school uniform was obligatory but could be expensive:

> When I passed my scholarship for the grammar school, mother applied for a grant towards my school uniform; I was given 7/6 which would have paid for the badge for my beret!

> Money was very tight and became apparent to me when I won a scholarship to a grammar school and realised that girls with Dads lived a different sort of life.

One contributor still remembers her badly fitting second-hand school uniform, another remembers her school blazer being bought at the Co-op where it was cheaper and her mother could collect a dividend. Unfortunately the colour of the garment was not the exact shade as the blazers bought at the nominated school outfitters, which was seemingly a trivial matter, but not to an eleven-year-old girl. Nora Lestrange left her grammar school aged fifteen in 1952 to take a job because her £2 a week wage was vastly more than the 11s child allowance her mother received.

It was often not possible to take part in extra-curricular activities, another thing which made the child of a war widow 'different' and children hate to be at variance with their peers. Betty Jennings was the only girl to stay at home when her classmates went on a school trip to the Festival of Britain in 1951 because her mother could not afford the required 2s 6d. Another recalls being selected to go on a trip to France because she was one of the best in the class at French; her mother was obliged to borrow the necessary funds from relatives. Cath Barnett was not aware that she lacked anything since they lived in what would be called a deprived area where everybody was in the same situation, until she went to grammar school in 1951:

> I realised that I was a 'deprived' child when I saw other girls with hockey outfits, tennis outfits, gym outfits etc. I, and a few others, didn't have such things and it was the first time I had two pairs of shoes, as we had to have a pair for outdoors and a pair for indoors... I didn't enjoy my time at Senior School.

These children were always aware that money was tight but accepted it as children do when they know nothing else. Children also accepted a parent's behaviour as normal because it was all they knew. Janet Stubbins says that her mother was very prone to 'nervous illness', but explains that she thought all mothers were like that, crying a lot and suffering from mood swings. The children of the impoverished war widow also knew that other children had swimming lessons, music lessons, pocket money and family holidays and they did not. Only one of our sample mentions a holiday other than staying with a relative: to a holiday home belonging to a school governor. For the fare to Devon her mother borrowed the money from SSAFA, money that she had to pay back a little at a time.

This sense of being 'different' does seem to have been common among the children of war widows. Some went even further and considered that other people looked down on them. Fran Whittle always felt different at school. Her mother had remarried but Fran retained her father's name and constantly had to explain that her father had died in the war. Sheila Cameron was the only child in her village to have lost her father. She remembers, as a seven-year-old being the only girl in the school not wearing a red, white and blue ribbon in her hair at the Victory celebrations. Her mother thought it 'inappropriate'. Ann Doward recalls feeling '…different and looked down upon by other children…' and never having a holiday until she had a job and was able to pay for it herself. Josephine Smith's father died when she was a mere thirteen months old; her mother remarried and now the only memento Josephine has of her father is a '… black and white photograph taken with my parents when I was a few months old …' and a letter written by the American captain who had buried her father. For some years she felt quite bitter at this apparent obliteration of her natural father. Post-war her father's old regiment informed her mother that his name was inscribed on the War Memorial in Bideford, North Devon but when the family later went to live in the area they never visited Bideford as her mother always said: '… there was nothing special to see; I believe she felt I would not then love my stepfather so things were hidden from me.'

One small boy was not to discover that his stepfather was not his real father until he was four years old. No doubt his mother thought she was doing the best for him and that he would not have understood at an earlier age. He was told reluctantly that his father had been a bomber pilot but whenever he asked any further questions he was fobbed off. It had the opposite effect; the boy became obsessed with knowing everything he could about his natural father but it was not until much later when his respected stepfather died that he ferreted out the truth: his father had in fact shot himself. A traumatic discovery for a teenage boy but he continued to pursue the matter and, despite his mother's continued opposition managed to track down his paternal grandparents.

Nonetheless he was always to be badly affected by this early experience and the cloak of mystery surrounding his father's life.

While the standard of living may have improved for the child of a widow who remarried, the situation was often fraught with other problems. Resentment perhaps of the attention going to the new spouse exacerbated when a stepbrother or sister arrived; the mother constantly being torn between the two factions. We have also had mention of a 'wonderful stepfather' and the relief of having a secure home life once again. It is difficult to make a judgement without comprehensive statistics but there certainly must have been many difficulties in these situations. One of the things such children regretted in later years was the loss of contact with their paternal grandparents.

Many the child of a war widow grew up with no memory of their father at all; he was just a picture on the sideboard:

> I have very few photographs of my father and only one of my mother, father and myself (aged about 12 months) together. It was taken on his last leave and my father took it with him to Burma in 1941. It came back, with his few effects, after his death. It is brown, spotted and creased and shows my mother smiling at the camera, but I am in my father's arms and he is smiling at me. I can hardly bear to look at this photograph because it shows what my life might have been had he lived. I have no memory of him at all but I often think how wonderful it would have been to grow up with a father who would have loved me.

> I know so very little about my father. In my parents' wedding photograph he is of middling height, quite slim and I believe he had brown hair and blue eyes. I don't remember anybody in my mother's family ever talking about my father. I did not see much of my father's family but, on those rare occasions, they never mentioned him either. I know nothing of his childhood or of his interests. I have no photographs of him as a child; he is a blank canvas. As a small child it was of little importance because I knew nothing else but, as I grew up, the absence of a father became increasingly more significant. My life would have

been very different had my father survived the war. I would have grown up in a family unit, probably with siblings. As it was there was always something missing. I greatly envied my friend whose father used to take her and her sisters out on bike rides, they always seemed to have fun.

My mother did her best. She encouraged me to join the library and we listened to the radio, especially to the Saturday night play, and she would take me to the cinema when she could. Education was very important to my mother and she was determined that I should do well at school. During the depression of the 1930s, with her father out of work, she herself had no option but to leave and go to work in a factory. She was resolved that I would not have to do the same thing. She impressed on me again and again that the only way to a better and more secure life was through education. The first step was to pass the examination for the Grammar School, which thanks to the 1944 Education Act was no longer fee-paying. The week before the momentous exam I fell in the playground and lost consciousness for a few minutes. There was no follow-up in those days and the schoolteacher assumed I had recovered. By the time I got home I had a dreadful headache which kept me bedridden for days. I was really unwell but, such was the importance of this exam to my mother, that I forced myself to go to school on the appointed day. My mother was thrilled when I passed but I did not particularly enjoy my time at Grammar School. I was the only girl in my class without a father and many of my fellow pupils were the children of professional people and had quite a different lifestyle.

My mother's family were very disapproving initially when I went to Grammar School and especially later when I stayed on to sit for the Higher School Certificate. They thought I should have left school at 15 and worked 'to bring in money'. My father's family expressed no opinion, when your father dies his family tend to be very much in the background. My mother was very much the 'poor relation' of her family. I suppose this was inevitable; they were prospering post-war but we stayed pretty much the same. My aunt used to pass down my cousin's dresses to me. Nothing wrong with that, except that these clothes were torn and soiled. My mother threw them out. I was entitled to free school meals but my mother paid to save me embarrassment. Our food at home was plain but there was always enough. I loved Sundays because I had a real egg for breakfast, the rest of the time we had dried egg in tins.

During the war my mother and I lived in my maternal grandmother's house together with my mother's sister and her small daughter. There were no men in the house. My grandfather was dead and the younger men were away in the Services. It was a house of women and I remember that when my aunt's husband came back from the war he had such a loud voice the first time he spoke to me that I ran away and hid.

I am now older than my mother was when she died. She lived to see and enjoy her own grandchildren but I wish she had had a better life. She was a widow for nearly 40 years, scrimping and saving during what should have been the best years of her life. She took poorly paid jobs to fit in with my school hours and holidays, never had a proper holiday herself and always put me first. I read somewhere about 'the unshared guilt of the only child' and I feel guilty that I have had such a good life compared with my mother's.

It was not unusual for the child of a widow to fantasise about the father they had never really known except from an old faded black and white photograph. If the photograph was of a man in uniform perhaps the greater the fantasy. They would imagine that their father was looking down on them and looking after them from above. All the hurts perceived and otherwise would have been prevented or assuaged had their father been alive. They too would have had a holiday at the seaside, a new bicycle for Christmas and endless treats. The possibilities are boundless in the mind of the fatherless child. Some children were kept in ignorance of a deceased father, accepting a stepfather as father because they had been too young to remember the real one and the mother thought it in the best interests of the child. The benefits are debatable, as most children are more aware than their parents realise. Particularly in the chaos of war with waves of troops passing through and constant movement of population, the marriage itself might have been a myth. It was not uncommon for an unmarried mother to take the easy option and let other people assume that she was a war widow. It was certainly easier for a growing child to accept. Sometimes the original marriage was acrimonious or perhaps the mother and father had already separated. Sometimes ignorance is bliss but not to the child desperate to know his 'real' father.

This feeling of isolation and of somehow being at variance with the majority is not confined to the children of British war widows. In America Ann Bennet Mix, who lost her father in the Second World War, founded the American WWII Orphans Network. It is open to any son or daughter of a serviceman killed or missing or who died as a result of wounds. On their website she explains her reasons for establishing this organisation:

I went through life not knowing that I was a 'war orphan'. I had heard that term – but I thought it referred to children who had lost both parents, probably in Europe, during the war. But the fact is that an orphan is anyone who has lost one or both parents, and a 'war' orphan is universally used by governments, including our own, as a term for children who have lost a parent in war. I learned I was an American 'war orphan' about the time I first began to want to find others like myself whose fathers had died in WWII. At that time I had no idea who they were, where they were or how many there were. When I turned to government agencies for help I discovered that they did not know either!

It was obvious there was a long struggle ahead, but I was determined that we come together and talk about our lives and what happened. As I started finding people and, as we did talk, I was angered and saddened to learn how few people had ever talked with another war orphan, or had been allowed to talk about their fathers. I learned that most of us had spent our lives feeling isolated, knew little about our fathers' service or how they died. Some had never even seen a photo of their Dad.

By checking veterans administrations statistics on benefits paid to war orphans I learned there had to be at least 183,000 children who were left fatherless as a result of WWII. I knew with greater surety that we needed to find each other, form a network all our own, and find out how to locate information about our fathers.

Since that time in 1991 when the American WWII Orphans Network was formed it has become a non-profit organisation, and has achieved national recognition from military, government and veterans' groups. We have located more than 1,000 sons and daughters of men who were killed – and many other family members. We have brought people together across the nation from Washington DC to Seattle, Washington and have also formed an online computer network of very active and sharing individuals from all over the United States.

No child wants to be different from his peers; a German soldier refused to marry his fiancée because having been a war orphan himself he knew what it was like and would not take the chance to bring another into the world. A dissertation on the aftermath of the Finnish wars states that: 'Nobody was interested in war orphans since, generally, they did not carry any signs of visible damage. How can you show that children miss their father?' For the war orphan the sense of being on the outside never goes away. When contemporaries reminisced about their childhood and family occasions that included a loving father they are yet again reminded of the great void in their lives. Perhaps it is even worse for the child who did have some recollection of a father. One such remembers sitting on a wall, crying, when other fathers came home from the war and hers did not. Roy Pickard also has specific memories of the festivities:

I remember (aged 10) the street tea parties held to celebrate the end of the war with Germany on VE Day in May 1945 and especially VJ Day to celebrate the end of the war with Japan in August 1945 because we thought that Dad would be coming home. I also remember other Dads coming home from the war, to their houses decorated with flags and a 'Welcome Home' sign, and still hoping to hear news of my Dad.

The following letter from Margaret Capon is particularly affecting:

> My beloved father was killed in Italy in Sept 1944. I was 9 years old, my brother 8 years and the youngest brother 2 years old. My mother sadly died just 2 years after my father in 1946. Her life had been a struggle all through the war, trying to pay the rent and look after us three children, even after the war she went cleaning to make ends meet... I and my brothers were sent to different relatives and never grew up together. At 11 years I had to grow up, no more childhood... After Mum's funeral which we weren't allowed to attend the three of us went to different relatives. I went to my Mum's brother and family near Rugby ... my cousins were younger, I was unhappy, children didn't mourn, no one cuddled you. Each week they had a comic each, not me. After three months I was sent to my Mum's sister and family to help with my young brother who was only 4 years old. He eventually ended up in a home and was adopted by a childless couple... From 11 years old I was no longer a child, nothing was ever the same again.

Now married for fifty-four years with three children and six grandchildren Mrs Capon goes on to say: 'At times I feel the little girl inside me crying and my tears fall, my husband gives me a cuddle, the cuddles I've missed from my parents.'

Mrs Willis vividly recalls taking the eleven-plus examination in floods of tears six weeks after her father's death and again, weeping at her own wedding many years later because her father was not there to give her away. Living in Plymouth during the war they were constantly subjected to heavy air raids. As she sat in the school air raid shelter her overwhelming fear was that her mother might be in danger outside and she would lose her too. Mrs June Burge's father was killed in Burma in 1944, writing in 2009 she says:

> The day my mother received that telegram stays with me to this day and I am now 71 years old... I was just 6 years old... I didn't like Christmas because most of the time Mum would hug me and keep telling me she was sorry that she wasn't able to buy me lots of things...

It was hard not having a dad around when you were little. When other kids used to talk about their dad it used to upset me... Life was a struggle for mum and me during those years, lots of heartaches and tears, no money but lots of love...

Children have far clearer memories of events than their parents give them credit for: Mrs Burge never forgot the day the telegram arrived. Another child, although only four years old at the time, always remembered the day in November 1939 when she and her family were listening to the radio together when the news came through that the armed merchant cruiser *Rawalpindi* had been sunk in the North Atlantic. *Rawalpindi* was the ship on which her father had been serving. For children already separated from their parents, in this case sent back to England to boarding school while their parents were stationed in India, the death of the father exacerbated the emotional gap, never to be filled.

We were all at different schools at the time of our father's death. Our ages when he died were 15 years, 13 years and I was 10 years old but we had not seen him for 5 years when he was recalled to India... I had very few memories of my father and my reaction was that he was now in heaven and would not have to take any more nasty medicine. I do not remember having any other thoughts... My sister dealt with it in her usual fashion by shutting it in on herself, she felt that the other girls found it embarrassing to talk to her ... she dreaded going home as she was not sure how our mother would cope... My brother Jeremy was 15 years old when his housemaster told him... He was about 10 years old when my father went back to India and he had built up a closer relationship with our father. On his last leave they had driven up to Scotland together to see where Daddy grew up... A few years ago Jeremy visited his grave where it had been moved to the Imperial War Graves Commission Kirkees Cemetery in the military cantonment in Poona. He found it a devastating experience.

Peter Michael Jewell's life was dramatically changed in every way when the Japanese took control of the International Settlement in

Shanghai on the fateful 8 December 1941. Peter lived there with his father, a master mariner with Jardine Matheson, and his mother who was a nursing sister. At the time of the takeover his two cousins were visiting from Hong Kong; they were to be trapped until the war ended in 1945. The occupants of the settlement were for some time confined to their residential areas and required to wear red armbands. Reports came through that his father had been killed and this was confirmed much later. Early in 1943 when Peter was ten years old all the settlement families were transported to Yangchow Prison Camp to the north of Shanghai; the journey itself must have been very frightening: first by ship then in barges along the Grand Canal, and into the unknown. Life in the camp was difficult, there were nine people living in the one room and food was never easy to come by, but everybody was in the same position. The camp held about 600 internees, among them sufficient teachers to run a school, even to set external exams, and Mrs Jewell was matron of the camp hospital:

...I believe a few individual punishments did take place (by the Japs) and, on occasion, mass punishment would involve standing on the parade ground, at attention, for an hour but this was fairly rare... As the years progressed it was evident that things were not going Japan's way. The military Commandant was replaced by a civilian, a mild man who could obviously see the inevitable outcome but food was getting short and the general health of the internees was deteriorating. Skinny? Believe it!

One day an aircraft flew over and circled the camp; it was a USAAF P-38 Lightning. Union Jacks appeared, and sheets laid out spelling POW brought no adverse reaction from the guards. Chinese locals were shouting over the wall that Japan had surrendered. Within a few days there was the first 'para drop' of food and medical supplies, much of which fell outside the camp. The Japanese guards escorted small groups to retrieve what they could. Subsequent drops were a lot more successful: double drums of canned fruit, chocolate, soups. If they had sent 'powerful' food like steaks etc it would probably have killed us. We had to be built up again, slowly, to be able to cope with normal food.

Liberated by American forces in 1945, Peter and his mother returned to their house in Shanghai. The house was intact, having been occupied by a Japanese officer and family in the interim. For a time Peter went back to school and his mother returned to nursing until 1947 when they were offered accommodation in England, near Nottingham, and through the influence of a friend in Shanghai, they were also offered a place for Peter at a boarding school in the same county. For him that transition was perhaps the greatest shock of all.

> We finally left Shanghai in August 1947 on the SS *Glen Artney* bound for Tilbury Docks and post-war London, rationing, food and clothing coupons, pea-soup fogs and the coldest winter on record. On the long sea voyage my mother became acquainted with another ex-internee who had been a government courier prior to the war. They set up home in London and I went to boarding school in Nottingham... A Public School of the old style, compulsory 'jump in' full submersion, cold bath every morning, bullying, beatings with a bamboo cane (by deputy Head-Master, House Master or Prefect depending on the perceived misdemeanour), dreadful food...

He had lost his father, his home and the life he had known. After two years in a prison camp he was now in a different prison in a strange land, and quite alone. A war orphan in every sense of the word.

Seven

THE WOMEN WHO MADE A DIFFERENCE

FOR MOST war widows the fact of their widowhood alone was about as much as they could cope with, often coupled with the struggle to provide for themselves and their children. But there were some who were not content to remain invisible and take whatever crumbs were thrown at them by successive governments and charitable organisations; this was the few who had the determination to fight the system and obtain justice for themselves and their suffering sisterhood.

First is Jessie Vasey, who we have already mentioned, because her initiative in Australia immediately after the Second World War helped get a just and reasonable system of support for war widows in that country. At the end of the Second World War there were some 10,000 Australian war widows (of approximately 680,000 servicemen, of whom 29,395 were reported killed or missing) mostly with young children and scattered throughout Australia, many of them isolated and lonely. At age forty-eight with two sons in the army, Jessie Vasey was to become something of a mother figure to these young women. She was not rich but she was clever, talented and well connected. Her fight was for justice for war widows – not handouts. Wherever possible she believed that they should help themselves, but she also believed that the state should enable these women to help themselves. It must be pointed out that there already existed two very efficient and comprehensive ex-servicemen's benevolent societies in Australia, which also concerned themselves with bereaved dependants, namely the Returned Servicemen's League (RSL), established in 1916 and very much in evidence to this day with 220,000 members and branches in virtually every township in Australia, and Legacy. Legacy was founded in 1923 and is equally wide-ranging and very supportive of the families of ex-servicemen. Currently (2010) the organisation is assisting 115,000 widows and 1,900 children and has 6,000 volunteers throughout Australia. Jessie Vasey's aim however was for something different: fellowship and self-help.

Based in Melbourne, Jessie initially placed advertisements in the local papers and held rallies in the Town Hall to gather in as many widows as possible: 300 turned up at the inaugural meeting. She acquired a meeting room for a nominal rent and by January 1946, had established a weaving craft guild, obtained a tutor and purchased looms with the battalion funds of disbanding regiments. Her primary aim, to bring together the sisterhood of widows, was thus achieved. Her second aim of self-help was also accomplished since the weaving they did was of professional standard, commercially viable and eagerly taken up by local stores at a time when there was a shortage of textiles. Thus the War Widows' Craft Guild, membership fee 1s, was established, first in Victoria and then state-by-state until by 1947 it covered the entire country and was re-named The War Widows' Guild of Australia. An astonishing achievement in so short a time.

Sadly Mrs Vasey encountered male prejudice in many forms, from men who simply viewed war widows as a nuisance, and also from men who, though sympathetic, wanted to do all the talking for them while the women understandably felt that they could speak for themselves. One government minister in 1947 referred to them as 'wretched flappers' even going so far as to cynically state: 'many of these flappers married these men in a hurry and a lot of them hoped they would never come back.' Jessie Vasey was herself called a 'battleaxe' and a 'warhorse', with some justification it would seem. But there was one public figure who showed his appreciation of their efforts in a very public manner. When

Field Marshal Montgomery visited Australia after the war he was given a civic reception in Melbourne. As his cavalcade wound its way through the city the Field Marshal, in his open car, spotted the banner of the War Widows' Guild hanging from their office window. He immediately sprang to his feet and saluted until his car had passed. Many years later widows still spoke of how moved they were by his very public recognition.

Mrs Vasey passionately believed in justice for all war widows, justice that she visualised as a pension commensurate with the minimum wage so that they had no need to go cap in hand asking for welfare benefits. She pointed out that had their husbands not made the ultimate sacrifice for their country these women could reasonably have expected a higher standard of living. By 1950 Jessie Vasey had turned the War Widows' Guild into the most powerful women's pressure group in Australia. Because war widows now spoke with one voice the Guild was so effective that politicians, despite their reluctance, could not afford to ignore them.

The Guild continually widened its remit. In *No Mean Destiny* Mavis Thorpe Clark relates how it managed – with help from RSL and others – to raise sufficient funds to provide specific housing for war widows and their families. The first specific accommodation for war widows and their families was bought in 1952 for £7,000, a great deal of money at the time. This was done initially by buying large older properties and converting them into flats then, later, on a larger scale with purpose-built housing. It was a tremendous undertaking but they were spurred on at all times by Jessie Vasey: 'Widows without decent homes are like the toad under the harrow, only the toad knows how it hurts.' Self-help was always the guiding principle of the guild; by 1985 it had been responsible for the development of 1,074 housing units for widows in need. She would have been honoured and delighted to know that today – in 2010 – in Melbourne they are still building Vasey Housing. Jessie Vasey died in 1963, having been the driving force behind so many of the improvements in the lot of the Australian war widow: better pensions, medical care and affordable housing to name a few. Above all she had given them a sense of worth.

In 1983 the Secretary of the New South Wales branch of the War Widows Guild addressed the World Veterans Federation in Nice in the following terms:

> Australian war widows are unique in the world and in no other country have war widows gained their rightful place in the community. Here we are united, honoured and respected by ex-service organisations and, most importantly by the Australian Government as able to speak for ourselves and so protect our statutory rights. Our programme of self-help has worked magnificently. War widows in countries such as Britain and the USA have tried to gain recognition but without success. They have no real voice – no real authority.

As we have learnt, when another Australian widow Laura Connelly moved to England in the 1950s she was horrified to learn that her widow's pension was subject to taxation and it was she in turn who set the ball rolling in the United Kingdom. Mrs Connolly went straight to the top, to the Conservative Prime Minister Edward Heath, in this instance. Her letter dated 3 August 1970 reads as follows:

> To whom it may concern at No. 10 Downing Street, London S.W.1
>
> Having asked a civil question (by letter) of the Prime Minister and, in reply, receiving a letter from one of his underlings, I would like to reciprocate the insult with a copy of the THOUGHTS such a letter evoked.

The 'thoughts evoked' – three and a half pages of single-spaced typing – are addressed to the 'Privileged Members of Society' and amount to a scathing attack on the way these persons of privilege acted towards unfortunates as the war widow whose pension, being classified as 'earned income' was subject to taxation. Subsequently one of these war widows had the insolence to ask 'How do I EARN this income?' Mrs Connolly's most vituperative cynicism was aimed at the members of the House of Lords: 'They are now able to collect £6 10s for each relaxing visit they make to the House, plus, of course, first-class travel there and back, with the further advantage, I might add (if they happen to be aged and dependent on the Welfare State) of being able to draw their Welfare State Retirement Pension ALL TAX FREE...' This she compares with one case raised in the House of Commons of an elderly war widow crippled by arthritis and living in a nursing home. The lady had a total income of £11 12s from which she paid £11 11s to the nursing home for her keep. Yet she had received an Income Tax demand for the year 1969–70 for £64 6s... 'After all she DID have a shilling left over, EVERY WEEK!'

That was only the beginning. Laura Connolly then embarked on a spirited correspondence with the Inland Revenue and one luckless official, a Mr McGivern with whom she had apparently spoken. (As mentioned elsewhere it was calculated that she owed the Inland Revenue £250.) The cut and thrust of their dialogue can be deduced from the following extracts:

(9 June 1971)

...If, as you have tried so hard to convince me, Mr McGivern, there is truly no difference between the accidentally killed civilian and the man who has died serving his country, what colossal hypocrisy has been practised for more than half a century, by the British Governments in erecting WAR MEMORIALS galore to those who died for their country; the 'Unknown Soldier' in the Abbey; the great Royal Parades round the Cenotaph year after year – to say nothing of the millions spent on war graves as a tourist attraction. Really!!...

(11 June 1971 to Mrs Connolly)

...As I explained during the recent interview it is clear that you can not be persuaded of the equity of the law as it applies to the taxation of war widows' pensions and I do not think it would help at all if I were to repeat again the reasons why successive Governments have never felt able to exempt these pensions from tax... I realise from what you have told me that you might not now be able to pay the arrears of tax which have accumulated since 1968 but I am not convinced that you could not pay your current tax liability. If I could see that you were paying regular amounts to the Collector sufficient to satisfy the tax which will become payable for this year, and of course future years, then I would be prepared to recommend to the Board that steps should not be taken to recover the arrears. Failing this however I am afraid that you would leave the Board with no option but to take whatever steps are open to them to collect <u>all</u> the outstanding tax, including if necessary bankruptcy proceedings.

(21 June 1971)

...I have no wish to be a martyr, but I do have a strong wish to see that the plight of war widows, and the anomalies in the taxation law relating to war pensions are, if possible, brought to light and rectified, and if there is no other way of doing this than my being 'put on the rack' as it were, well, so be it. Please go ahead and do whatever you wish.

(7 July 1971 to Mrs Connolly)

...You have not replied to the point I raised in the last paragraph of my letter of 11 June and as this will determine the Board's action I must ask you to let me have a clear answer one way or the other.... I said in my earlier letter that I appreciated that you might not be able to pay the arrears of £250 odd but I was not convinced that you could not pay current and future tax liabilities. So that we both know precisely where we stand will you please let me know whether you are prepared to commence paying regular weekly payments or monthly sums in respect of the tax of £106.56 and to continue payment of any tax which may be due for future years without imposing any conditions about the law as it relates to the taxation of war widows' pensions...

(22 July 1971)

...I cannot believe that you were not writing with your tongue in cheek when you suggest: '... and to continue payment of any tax which may become due for future years without imposing any conditions about the law as it relates to war widows' pensions.' I am amazed that any normal person could make such a suggestion to one who has battled

against all the odds of the prevaricating letters, from endless governments, <u>for more than ten years;</u> during which time I submitted to
the unjust law by paying out hundreds of pounds in tax. Then, after I
decided, more than two years ago, to take a firm stand on the matter in
order to bring the issue to a head I have been subjected to nothing but
dire harassment beginning with the usual 'frightening' letters – month
after month –with threats of 'Distraint' and 'Court Proceedings'...

(31 July 1971 to Laura Connolly)

...I note you have decided not to accept the offer made in my letter of
7 July and I am afraid that you leave me no alternative but to continue
recovery proceedings for the whole of the outstanding tax. The Board's
solicitor is being instructed to institute bankruptcy against you and a
bankruptcy notice will be issued to you shortly. I am sorry it has come
to this but your actions leave no other course open to the Board.

(3 September 1971)

...I would point out that I am NOT INSOLVENT. I am a responsible
citizen who abides by every JUST law of the land... My character
is such that a bribe of £250 million could not buy my support for
INJUSTICE, let alone £250. In worldly endowments I am poor so,
owing to the expense, it would be impossible for me to engage a solicitor who could, or would, cope with the insidious double-talk of those
employed by a government that is determined to operate unjust laws...

Laura Connolly's case and that of 'Britain's Forgotten Women' was
eagerly taken up by the press and an article detailing her story
appeared in a Sunday newspaper in September 1971. At seventy-
nine years of age Laura displayed remarkable energy, firing letters
off in all directions; her letters to the press generated an enormous correspondence. True, her daughter helped her, but she
does seem to have replied individually to all of them. To offers of
help from other widows she sometimes sent a duplicated letter
but always with a personal footnote. This letter was sent to a Mrs
Lorimer (who was to become the first Secretary of the WWA) on
18 September 1971:

Do PLEASE excuse this duplicated letter ... but I have received so many encouraging, and at the same time, heartrending letters with regard to my stand against the taxing of war widows' pensions that I cannot cope with replying personally straight away, but I do want you to know how I appreciate your writing to me with all your good wishes for my success.

A lady up in Liverpool has put forward the idea that all widows should put on some kind of demonstration on Remembrance Day – MOST appropriate I should think. It has been suggested that we get in touch with the British Legion. I have done this, but I have heard since that to expect anything from them is completely hopeless. From my personal experience the same can be said of M.P.s. I wonder if I could persuade you to write to the *Sunday Express*? If we could swamp them there we might get more favourable publicity. At the moment the Kentish papers are taking it up...

Another missive dated two weeks later is addressed 'Dear Staunch Supporter':

...What we are HOPING to do is arrange a QUIET demonstration on Remembrance Day. BUT, you dear ladies need not worry that we will call on you to do anything. We are going to get women around London who will be willing to represent you. We are going to get in touch with the big shops, tell them our story, and ask them to donate a yard or two of cheap black material and black voile. I will then run these up into veils and cloaks, so the women's faces won't be seen. A friend is making placards to wear on our backs. On them will be printed an indication of the Government's treatment of war widows. About a dozen women will stand round the Cenotaph – facing it – with placards facing Whitehall, for about fifteen minutes, and then take the placards off and place them among the wreaths and just walk away. Of course we will warn the press we are going to do it with the hope of getting photographers there...

Again dated 9 October:

...Thanks to the *Sunday Express* which sparked off our 'Cause' we are now beginning to 'surface' in our fight for justice. We want to do what is best and what will be most effective... For instance we have HINTED to Inland Revenue what MIGHT happen on Remembrance Sunday... I am continually being rung up by the press asking me to be sure to let them know 'when you get IT' and I feel strongly that a few, good, sympathetic journalists in the court can do far more for our Cause than all the marches and demonstrations in the world...

All this time Mrs Connolly was still battling with the Inland Revenue. She writes again to Mrs Lorimer on 18 November:

...The bankruptcy notice was delivered by hand, <u>11am</u> on the 11th November – the irony of it! ... My main thought has been, ever since I started to fight, if I only make <u>one</u> aging, defenceless woman happy, when I have won this fight, I will be repaid for these many years of effort and expense I have put in ... I have already enjoyed nearly a decade beyond the allotted span of life so it little matters what the Inland Revenue if, in the end, some other woman, or maybe MANY women are allowed to have less worries in their declining years. I am no martyr ... but I will fight this out till I drop, I will <u>not</u> give in NOW...

Among the numerous responses from other war widows was one from Jill Gee. If Laura Connolly was the catalyst for change it was Mrs Gee who picked up the baton and was to found the WWA. Her open letter to the newspapers appeared with the rallying cry:

Three cheers for Mrs Connolly who at 79 years of age is prepared to go to prison rather than pay an unjust tax on her War Pension... I think I speak for all War Widows when I say that Armistice Day in this country is a hypocrisy. Our men would prefer you to honour their wives. We are still suffering the penalties and injustices their deaths brought. If everyone would devote two minutes each day to thinking about what we had to face (with even leaner years ahead) perhaps we could be helped in our fight for justice. If not we, the War Widows, must take the advice of a grand old lady of 79 and fight alone – after all we have been doing it for years... We must march in protest if Bankruptcy Proceedings are commenced against Mrs Connolly. Indeed November 11th would be an appropriate day. The forgotten 14th Army eventually gained recognition. Perhaps it is not too late for recognition to be given to the Forgotten War Widows.'

Jill Gee had been widowed in 1944 when her husband, a pilot-captain in the Royal Artillery, was killed. Eight months later her daughter was born. In common with the majority of war widows she had to work to supplement her pension but found that, because her pension was added to her salary for tax purposes, her take-home pay was less than that of the office juniors. After fares and lunches were deducted she did not have enough to pay the baby-minder. Eventually she took advantage of an opportunity to live in America where the war pension was considered an ex-gratia payment and nursery schooling was provided for the children of men killed in the war. She was even able to save a little money. Two years later she returned to England to find nothing had changed: the widow's pension was still counted as earnings for tax purposes.

She continued her protests but until the publicity surrounding Laura Connolly's case had made little headway. The refusal of successive British governments to release the names of war widows, for perfectly legitimate reasons, had made it difficult for any national organisation. There were local associations, particularly in garrison towns and ports but nothing on a countrywide scale. Jill Gee's initiative in forming the WWA in January 1972 gave war widows a forum where they could express their legitimate grievances. It was the first vital step in a long and difficult struggle. As chairman, Mrs Gee's first official communication dated 1 February 1972 went to Prime Minister Edward Heath and all 629 other MPs. It was a dignified yet impassioned plea for justice:

The War Widow's pension was earned by a young man leaving his chosen career to fight in order to save Britain from destruction. The

object was achieved through the sacrifice of human life and the ending
(in many cases) of what promised to be a brilliant future; certainly
it ended the right of a man to provide adequately for his dependants. Due to the war he was unable to insure against death – and no
Government sponsored insurance was offered to him.

She condemned the 'pathetic inadequacy' of the British War
Widow's Pension, contrasting it with provision in other countries,
particularly Germany 'the defeated country' where a war widow
received £88.48 per month tax-free. In the USA the pension was
£30 weekly, while in Australia and France generous tax-free pensions were combined with low interest loans and free travel. In
her letter she went on to demolish the Treasury statement that
'India taxes her war widows' with the scathing observation that
'India has also burnt her war widows! Regrettably many of them
now die on the pavements'. She pointed out the extra burden for
widows with children:

The strain of having full responsibility – morally and financially – for
such children caused severe mental stress to Britain's War Widows.
Hers could never be a 'two income' family, yet a married woman
was given special concessions when working (we are told) IN THE
NATION'S INTERESTS... The War Widows of Gt. Britain continue to
suffer the penalties, hardships and injustices their sacrifices brought,
and have done so for most of their adult lives unlike a Widow whose
husband has died under normal circumstances, in the main at an age
when her partner has had time to make his way in life and provide
a home...

Sadly this letter like many others that followed failed to convince
the authorities though several letters refer to the sympathetic
stance regarding war widows' pensions taken by Admiral Lord
Mountbatten in his letter to The Times of 4 November 1971: 'It is
painful to sit here and realise we are behind every Commonwealth
country in the treatment of War Widows.' One lady wrote to thank
him and received a reply stating his intention to take the matter

up again with the Secretary of State for Social Services on behalf of the British Commonwealth Ex-Services League. Undeterred, Jill Gee continued to campaign, employing every approach she could think of to get publicity and raise the profile of the WWA at a time when the general public were mostly ignorant of the shameful tax on war widows' pensions. She was constantly urging her members to write directly to their own MPs to bring to their attention nuggets of information such as the fact that a German war widow could live in Britain if she chose, yet would pay no tax on her German war pension.

Unknown to the members of the WWA Mrs Gee was herself under considerable financial pressure. Using a small legacy from her mother to subsidise her pension she had left work in order to devote her time and energy to the WWA and the legacy was soon gone. Nevertheless she continued to write endless letters of encouragement to her fellow members, many of whom felt themselves to be on the margins of society. She understood and sympathised with their problems as is illustrated in the following letter to a woman whose husband was killed when the war was almost at an end:

> There were no celebrations for us when the war ended. We just got what Churchill had promised 'Blood, tears, toil and sweat' – and this continues – One of the arguments the powers-that-be present is that if tax on war widows was abolished it would help the 'better off' war widows. What a pity they do not show the same concern for the Peers (many millionaires) receiving a tax free income for sitting three days [weekly] in the House. And, if those who are better off benefitted, what of it – they can never be compensated for the loss of one to share their joys and sorrows with...

Jill Gee particularly reached out to those isolated widows who had never before been part of any organisation. By involving as many as possible in an active campaign she gave them motivation and hope for the future. She is commemorated with a paving stone in the National Arboretum and by a dedicated bench in the grounds of Liverpool Cathedral. Her lasting legacy is the WWA as it is today, an organisation of influence.

Much of the material for this book has come from the Iris Strange Collection. As previously mentioned, Iris was a war widow whose husband Robert was taken prisoner at Singapore in February 1942 and died in captivity. His body was never found and his death was not affirmed by the War Office until 1946 when his widow was awarded the basic £1 weekly widow's pension plus 7s for her son Tony. Unable to exist on this paltry sum she was obliged to find outside work and, when all other options failed, put her son into an orphanage. To her great distress Tony grew up believing that she did not want him and on leaving school, instead of returning home, he enlisted in the Fleet Air Arm. Tragically he was killed aged twenty-three and, although Tony had eventually understood his mother's motives for seemingly abandoning him, Iris never forgave the miserly government responsible:

> Had I been able to make a home for him instead of being forced to send him away I would no doubt have been enjoying my grandchildren now as well as my son, and governments are to blame for this tragedy as well as [for] the thousands of other calamities which have befallen war widows through being abandoned by those who owe us so much...

In 1971 she heard Jill Gee in a radio broadcast promoting the proposed WWA. Mrs Strange immediately joined and was later to become its Secretary, a post she held for ten years. She kept all the correspondence – official and otherwise – during her tenure and when she died in 1992 all her papers in forty-seven boxes were given to Staffordshire University where they are known as the Iris Strange Collection. Both in her capacity as Secretary to the WWA and personally, Iris never ceased to badger politicians and other people of influence. She had high hopes of Margaret Thatcher and was grateful when during her administration in 1979 war widows' pensions became entirely tax-free.

She now turned her attention to another project which she had been mulling over for some time as is apparent from a letter she wrote in 1977 to David Jacobs, then compering the programme 'Any Answers'. She outlined the fate of many elderly lonely widows with no family to care for them and no option but to linger on in a council care home:

> For the past two years it has been my urgent desire that when I retire in a little over a year I should do my best to open up a suitable place especially for elderly war widows, and make as many places as possible for those with no family. I visualise such an establishment being manned by those of us who are able-bodied... I know that to obtain such a place in the beginning would need a vast amount of money ... but I know of one or two members, myself included, who would be willing to sell their small but valuable homes to help raise the money.

Nothing is that simple; it took Iris more than a year and endless long letters to get the so-called Rainbow Trust registered as a charity. It was not until 1979 that she was actually able to launch a direct appeal for funds. Her aim was to buy a large house and convert it into bedsits; she hoped, perhaps optimistically, that it would be staffed by younger, fitter war widows. It was doubtful that that particular aspect of the proposals would ever have worked! This was all very reminiscent of Jessie Vasey's efforts in Australia but nowhere in Iris' substantial correspondence does she refer to the Australian enterprise. She did visit a Cheshire Home to see how things could be organised. Cheshire Homes were founded by the late Group Captain Leonard Cheshire initially to care for those left incurably ill by their experiences in the Second World War.

In 1979 the fundraising was certainly alongside that of the WWA, since a newspaper reported that £40 had been raised for the trust at the 'association's midsummer social meeting'. Nevertheless Iris was at pains to point out in her newsletters that the Rainbow Trust for War Widows was a separate organisation. Her energy was astounding and she even found time to compose a poem:

The days of our youth were brief my love.
The call to arms cut short our dream.
The joys that should have been ours my love
Were killed by your sacrifice supreme.

Did anyone care for us, my love,
For the ones you left behind?
No one cared for us, my love,
We were left to a long, hard grind.

We have been unable to discover any further details about the Rainbow Trust. The project seems to have fizzled out; from the monies collected, a number of small grants were made but the housing programme never materialised.

There was soon another can of worms however, and that, as we have previously discussed, was the additional pension given to war widows of the later conflicts in Northern Ireland and the Falklands. Iris Strange lost patience with the lack of progress in achieving parity for all war widows and with the WWA's approach to this issue. Sadly there were also clashes of personality within the committee, with some members objecting to the simultaneous fundraising for both the WWA and the Rainbow Trust and the anomalies that this created. Iris could certainly be abrasive, and her single-mindedness and lack of deference to the establishment was bound to create difficulties within a set-up such as the WWA. Consequently she resigned altogether from the WWA and formed the breakaway British War Widows and Associates (BWWA). She summarises this action in a letter dated 7 November 1985 to a member of the Royal Air Force Association:

All was well until we became infiltrated by a handful of well-heeled women who were more concerned with a social life than with the work for which we had formed the association. After two years of frustration and seeing the money of desperately poor war widows being wrongly used I resigned.

There was lots more regarding 'rigged' elections of officers but we only have Iris Strange's version of this and there may have been other explanations. While the WWA was now recognised to be on a par with the respectable and well established service and ex-servicemen's organisations, the BWWA, influenced by Iris, took on an increasingly militant attitude. As Hon. President/Secretary she continued to press for parity for all war widows through the medium of radio, television, petitions, newspaper articles and, above all, by acrimonious and abusive letters to the Prime Minister and her administration. In the hope of shaming them into action she compiled a dossier of harrowing letters and sent them to MPs, the press and whomever else she could think of who might have some influence:

My husband was killed in 1942 and I was left with a child under three years old and given the princely sum of 36/- a week and a piece of paper to say how proud I should be that my husband had made the ultimate sacrifice. To this day I am not. I had no home so my boy, at eight, had to go into a Home. He came home at holidays and then went to a RN boarding school at eleven, so I missed my son's childhood.

I was married three weeks before war broke out to a Chief Officer on a Merchant Ship. We went down with his ship on December 8th [1939] but it was February before I was awarded a pension of £100 per year. Probate was refused because I could not produce a death certificate and all his assets were frozen, including our joint bank account, although some of that money was mine. When I found I was pregnant I asked if there was any possibility of more money until the baby was born, but was curtly told if I could not manage on the pension I had better apply for Parish Relief. I preferred to go back to work as a Pharmacist though it meant standing all day and, in the midst of a 'flu epidemic, not getting home until 10 pm. I developed toxemia and the baby was born six weeks premature, stillborn. So all I had lived for those past seven months had gone and it seemed there was nothing left, and all because I had to work for lack of a decent pension on which I could live and the red tape of the freezing of my husband's estate.

My husband was a prisoner in the last war for five years as a result of which he died. I am unable to claim Social Security as I am 73p. above the limit. I work in the summer for exactly four months. For this I pay £89 tax.

My husband was a FEPOW [Far East Prisoner of War] and has been deceased for eight years, but previous to this he was a very sick man and I had to nurse him for a number of years, but I really don't think there is anyone who troubles about any of these men's sufferings. They did their job for their country and, as far as I can see, the widows are forgotten.

...he was 100% disabled but he died in 1977, February 3rd aged 60, that's when my nightmare began. I had just lost my dearest husband... I was glad he wasn't alive to see me go through the terrible ordeal I went through... I was sat there in a room in front of a big table with all the top doctors and was told I wasn't going to get a war widow's pension.

Despite her efforts the government remained obdurate and Iris' frustration was reflected in her frequently censorious letters to the powers that be. As for example in 1983 when the family of Flight Lieutenant James Nicolson decided to sell his Victoria Cross – the only one awarded during the Battle of Britain – to raise money for his widow and to highlight the plight of all war widows. The sale of Flight Lieutenant Nicolson's VC also prompted Air Vice-Marshal (retired) Charles Maugham to write in a similar vein to *The Sunday Times* on 6 March 1983:

No one surely should have to sell medals to maintain themselves and it is a mark of national shame when a war widow finds it necessary to do so... There are around 70,000 war widows today the majority having lost their husbands in World Wars I and II. It is they who are suffering most from the lack of support which the nation spontaneously accorded to those who fell in the Falklands... The gap in income between the elderly war widows who are least able to cope and the younger widows should be closed.

The Piper Alpha disaster of 1988 (when an oil rig off the Scottish coast caught fire and 167 men lost their lives) was to trigger yet another spate of angry letters, this time with reference to the Prime Minister's remark that: 'it is unthinkable that the bereaved should have any money worries.' Iris considered this an insult to those war widows fighting so hard for parity of pensions. In Mrs Thatcher's defence, it must be said that despite her refusal to grant this parity, she genuinely believed that her government had done more for war widows than any of her predecessors. Iris continued the attack:

> ...men who work on oil rigs accept the risks for the very high rates of pay and for the extremely generous compensation paid to their families ... our men did not rush to defend this country for high pay, they were probably the lowest paid of any fighting men during two World Wars and certainly we have been the lowest paid war widows. You refuse to listen to my pleas for help for war widows and you sent me replies that are a disgrace to the country... We know that the day the last war widow dies there will be rejoicing in Downing Street.

In some societies such letters would have the writer carted off to prison but, as ever, Iris received the usual stonewall reply from the Private Secretary to the Parliamentary Under Secretary for Social Security. Undaunted, she continued in the same vein, harassing the government at every opportunity, enlisting the help of MPs and exploiting every avenue of publicity. She did this to such an extent that she was constantly being asked for comments by the press who were under the erroneous impression that she was still on the committee of the WWA, which was an impression that Iris did nothing to dispel. That she was held in high regard by members of her BWWA was never in doubt, and when the government finally conceded parity in 1989 (to take effect from 1990) one of her supporters wrote to her:

> Now at last people are hearing our voices. Thank you from all the neglected widows. You have been a rock for us to lean on all these years.

Iris never ceased to work to promote justice for the sisterhood. On her death in July 1992 Nicholas Winterton MP recorded:

> There can be no doubt that Iris Strange has materially improved the lives of tens of thousands of war widows who have benefitted directly from her tenacious campaign to bring about a significant improvement in their pensions and to which she dedicated her boundless energy for so many years.

In her obituary Christopher Whitehouse wrote in *The Independent*:

> ...For half a century war widows had survived on the most meagre of incomes, and deprived of the opportunity to share in the years of prosperity which followed the Second World War, were not able to provide adequately for their later years. A meeting 10 years ago between Iris Strange and the Conservative MP Nicholas Winterton led to the inauguration of the All-Party Parliamentary Group for pre-1973 War Widows which went on to become the vehicle for parliamentary action on their behalf. Strange had severed her links with the more established War Widows' Association slightly earlier. This made her unpopular with many ex-service organisations who never forgave her for a step which ultimately embarrassed them into supporting her cause. Through the all-party group Mrs Strange established links with politicians from both Houses of Parliament. She channelled her considerable energies into a dogged attempt to persuade them to take up her cause. The more successful she was, the more she was isolated by other organisations, and it was not until victory was in sight that they finally gave her the support she deserved.
>
> The campaign for a fair deal for war widows had its price. It cost the government £100m per year, once the cause had been won, and led to an attack by the government whips upon Winterton's integrity. It even saw Iris Strange stand accused by the Government Chief Whip of having forged a letter from Margaret Thatcher's office in 1974 which purported to commit the Conservative Party to tackling this problem. Time has passed and Iris Strange's name has been cleared of this

calumny, but she still paid dearly. The campaign cost her all her time, energy and resource for over 15 years. It became her life.

Another lady who was never content to accept the status quo was Elizabeth (Betty) Tebbs. Betty had worked in a paper mill from the age of fourteen; her pay for a five and a half day week was 10s 6d, yet a boy doing the same job got 13s. She joined the Trade Union which, unusually for the time, had a women's branch at the mill. Her boyfriend Ernest's sister later became area organiser (known as 'Mother of the Chapel') and was much admired by Betty who at eighteen years old initiated her own first industrial action. On that particular occasion it failed, but her interest in the Trade Union movement was anchored.

As mentioned earlier she married Ernest Whewell after a five year courtship, then in 1940 he went into the army and in 1942 a daughter, Patricia, was born. Ernest saw his daughter on only three occasions before his death in 1944. As a widow, Betty's allowances were drastically reduced but her commitments were the same. She writes:

> I realised that there are two things that could be done in situations such as this, one is to succumb, and the other to fight back... I vowed I would work for peace for the rest of my life. The War had politicised many people and my circumstances heightened my political interests.

Betty went back to work at the paper mill, bitterly resenting the level of income tax she had to pay. Coincidentally she had become acquainted with the man who was to become her second husband on his demobilisation from the army in August 1946. Len Tebbs was an ardent socialist and reader of the *Daily Worker* and, coached by him, Betty became increasingly of the same mind. Both disgusted with the ongoing British anti-Communist action in Malaya they joined the Lancashire Bury and Radcliffe branch of the Communist Party in the 1950s. Len was a great influence in Betty's life, giving her freedom of action and, at the same time, all the emotional and practical support she needed. Betty immediately took an active part in pursuing the party's agenda, collecting signatures for the Stockholm Peace Appeal and illegally coating walls with 'Ban the Bomb' slogans.

She had given birth to a son, Glyn, in 1947, and later worked at a different paper mill where she gradually talked many of the other female employees into joining the union and was involved in her first official strike. From that time Betty became totally engaged with the union movement, becoming 'Mother of the Chapel', district representative and member of the district committee and of the Radcliffe Trades Council. She was involved in an acrimonious demonstration to Parliament protesting unemployment, termed 'a mob' by the media. She was elected the union's women's representative for the north-west and in 1958 attended the annual conference at Scarborough, and again in 1960 where she put forward a proposal to demand the withdrawal of American forces from bases in Britain.

Betty Tebbs moved up through the trades union hierarchy, albeit with a few hiccups, and in the 1960s was selected to represent the union at an International Women's Conference in Switzerland. In 1963, the year of the marriage of her daughter Pat, against tough opposition she also got herself elected onto the Radcliffe Local Council. As she wrote in her autobiography:

> I was now busier than ever. I was chair of the local Labour Party, vice chair of the Health Committee, chair of the Library Committee, Governor of the local grammar school and a primary school, a member of the Old People's Welfare Committee.

Husband Len was also hard at work, getting academic qualifications while still in employment. When he got a teaching job in Cheshire Betty reluctantly moved house, leaving the mill job and all her extra-curricular activities behind. She had never been simply a housewife and finding the inactivity very trying, she soon got herself a job at a local bag factory where, she had been informed, the women had minimal TUC representation. With wages a fraction of her previous salary she needed no persuasion and soon once more became 'Mother of the Chapel'. While attending a shop stewards course at Congress House she met Vic Feather, then General Secretary of the TUC.

Politics are never that cut and dried however. Len and Betty, who had both resigned from the Communist Party in 1956 over disagreement of policy, now became disillusioned with local Labour Party politicking and left that party too. They rejoined the Communist Party, while continuing to be very active locally and on behalf of their respective trades unions. For example they organised a petition protesting a proposed Council House rent rise of 30s weekly and did manage to get the sum reduced. Betty attended the 1968 TUC Conference as a delegate from the Newton-Le-Willows branch and succeeded in getting the conference to agree to a Women's Advisory Committee, despite the consternation of the many male union 'die-hards'. All along her crusade was to get women equal pay for equal work.

During the 1960s and '70s Betty switched jobs a number of times; she was variously delivering bread for the Co-op, invoice clerk in a paint works and canteen assistant in a factory. Feeling the need for more formal qualifications she signed up for a course in Industrial Relations at Middlesex Polytechnic which of course meant rooming in London and naturally – being Betty – she carried on being involved politically in whatever protest or demonstration was afoot. Because Len's health was not good after previously suffering a heart attack, she decided after the first year to transfer to Liverpool Polytechnic, a college closer to home. From the first she was at loggerheads with the economics tutor and she did not enjoy the Liverpool experience; she left at the end of that year.

Home again she became very involved with the Warrington Branch of the National Assembly of Women (NAW) and with it the setting up of a refuge for battered women. In 1977 she was asked to represent the NAW at the Working Women's Conference in Hungary. There were to be a great many more overseas trips as the NAW was affiliated to the Women's International Democratic Federation and Betty Tebbs, as sometime chair of the NAW, frequently represented that organisation. During the 1980s, particularly following Len's death, she travelled to meetings in Finland, Italy, Bulgaria, Switzerland, Kenya, Ireland and Geneva. Among the highlights of her political life were no doubt addressing the TUC conference in 1969 and speaking to 3,000 women in the Lenin Stadium in Moscow in 1986 at the invitation of Valentina Tereshcova, the pioneering spacewoman and member of the Central Committee of the Communist Party.

Betty has never ceased to pursue her political activities be they anti-nuclear, pro-peace, the fight for equality or simply fighting any system she believes to be unjust. Her crusade was undoubtedly set in motion by the meagre support given to her after her first husband's death in action. As she said at a speech celebrating National Women's Day in 1993: 'No one says working for peace is easy. But we have no choice if we are to save for future generations the planet we inherited.' In 1997 – aged seventy-nine – she picketed the BBC for broadcasting an election speech by the British National Party. Nor has she ever ceased to believe that socialism and peace go hand in hand as is illustrated by her arrest in 2007 for demonstrating outside a military base in Scotland. In 2010 aged ninety-two she was presented with the Elizabeth Gaskell Award by Manchester City Council. We salute her.

CONCLUSION

WHEN IT comes down to it, the principal thrust of this book is government attitudes to the financial support of its widows from two world wars. Almost every other aspect (apart from the trauma of widowhood itself of course) of a widow's emotional and physical well-being seems to stem from that fact. During the First World War some 770,000 British men died for their country. (It is difficult to name an exact figure because sources differ.) For the Second World War the estimated figure is 160,000. Many more men would later lose their lives from their disablement, mental as well as physical; they are not included in these figures. How many of these men were married is impossible to quantify but perhaps we can make an educated guess of one third to half of them. In 1945, at the end of the war, there were 212,427 widows in this country, and by 1990 when most of their financial problems had been worked out, there were 52,713.

Viewed impartially it is understandable that consecutive governments after the Second World War, the period with which we are principally concerned, were so tight-fisted. It took the British a long time to pull themselves up after the war and it was not until the 'swinging sixties' was there any appreciable rise in the standard of living – all the new council houses had bathrooms – but Britain was still bedevilled by miners' strikes and social unrest and there was the American debt to be serviced. In addition, these years could hardly be termed peaceful: the Cold War was ongoing, there were military actions in Palestine, Malaya and Korea where some 1,000 British soldiers had lost their lives, there were also incursions at Aden and the beginnings of the Northern Ireland conflict. In 1982 the United Kingdom's military honour was challenged by the Falklands affair, in 1992 British forces were involved in Iraq and at present our forces are engaged in Afghanistan. Each round of hostilities inevitably results in another cluster of war widows. How does the current treatment of these women compare with that of earlier times?

It may seem that we have in this book concentrated too much on the financial aspect of widowhood since the first three chapters are concerned with pensions. To be a war widow is tragic enough but to have to struggle for every penny compounds the tragedy. We are not talking about the more comfortably off war widow, because we had very little input from those with independent incomes. We are discussing the vast majority of war widows and that includes many officers' wives whose husbands held wartime commissions but may have come from modest backgrounds. For most war widows the war widows' pension was the sole income. To bring it up to a living wage they had to find outside work. If there were children the work had to be fitted in around the children's needs, hence the predominance of low-paid unskilled jobs.

Writing in 1924, Eleanor Rathbone, that women's champion, quotes a statement in *The Nation*:

> A correspondent wrote to *The Times* in alarm the other day to say that if all soldiers' widows were to have pensions that would keep them, the upper classes would soon find themselves short of servants.

The impression that correspondents gave (generally the widows themselves or their children) is that these women had almost literally to 'work their fingers to the bone'. Any additional expense above the norm (the school uniform is often cited) and they were completely thrown; possibly the only option was to appeal to a charity for the shortfall. The widows living with family were the most fortunate – if such a term can be used – they at least had a roof over their heads. Before the National Insurance Act came into force in July 1948 becoming ill was another nightmare as the doctor's fee might take up most of a week's pension. The war widows' pension was surely her prime concern; it was a matter of survival.

A great deal of the material in this book comes from the Iris Strange Collection at Staffordshire University. Apart from the work of Janis Lomas, this was the only substantial source of information we were able to find. Iris Strange was a very forceful woman and her sole aim was always to get a decent income for every war widow; if she offended anybody while pursuing that aim it did not matter one jot. For obvious reasons we cannot know the items of correspondence she chose not to keep, some of which may well have put quite a different slant on her efforts. On the other hand it also proves that she did get a lot of support from both the general public and assorted prominent citizens.

As we have said before we have found almost no literature concerned with British war widows in the twentieth and twenty-first centuries but quite a few works on the social and economic aspects of widowhood in general. There are frequent references to the higher pensions of war widows compared to the '10s widows' of the intermediate and immediate post-war years. They were not that high however: in the 'swinging sixties' the childless widow of a private was still in receipt of the princely sum of £1 per week. When parity for all war widows was agreed in 1990 the civilian widow's pension was about £8 per week less than that of the war widow but – and a big but – the former could claim a raft of additional benefits not available to a war widow. The only concession available to the latter was that the first £4 of the pension might be disregarded for general rating purposes at the discretion of the local council. Imagine the nightmare of form filling for any widow seeking additional financial support in a system inevitably predisposed to interpretation. (Iris Strange did once observe that although they didn't get much help from governments she had always found War Pensions Welfare Officers very sympathetic and helpful.)

Today the war widow's financial situation is certainly much improved, to quote the official jargon:

> ...in 2005 the Armed Forces Pension Scheme [AFPS] was introduced alongside the Armed Forces Compensation Scheme [AFCS] The spouse or recognised partner of those who die an attributable death post April 2005 receive a Guaranteed Income Payment from the AFCS and a Forces Family Pension.

The War Pensions Scheme is now administered by the Service Personnel and Veterans' Agency, an Executive Agency of the Ministry of Defence. As of 2010–11 the basic war Widow's Pension is paid at two rates, Standard to a widow over forty years of age, or under forty and childless, and Lower a widow under forty with no children. The Standard Rate for widows of other ranks is £117.30 per week; the Lower a mere £28.10s. For the widows of officers the Standard Rate commences at £6,189 per year rising to £6,239 according to rank. The Lower Rate begins at £1,699 and rises to £2,167. In addition Age Allowances are paid at ages sixty-five, seventy and eighty. These range from yearly allowances of £699 to the widows of officers and weekly allowances of from £13.40 to the widows of other ranks. Children's Allowances are paid annually to officers' widows at the rate of £960 for the first child and £1,075 for other children. To the widows of other ranks the weekly allowance is £18.43 and £20.60. There is actually these days very little difference between the pensions and allowances of officers and other ranks.

On 23 March 2010 there was a letter in *The Times*:

> WORTH 358 WIDOWS?
>
> Sir,
>
> A war widow with a six-year-old son receives a pension of £6000 and each MEP costs £2,150,000 (reports March 22nd). As a society have we lost the plot?

We have seen that women react in different ways to the death of a young husband in war. Some – understandably – go to pieces, some seek security and remarry when the opportunity arises but a surprising number tough it out, which was especially the case if there was already a child. This lady, writing to us in 2010, was one such:

> I just had the one child. She had the best I could afford. She went to a grammar school and her whole life has been a joy to me. I have never been one to bemoan my lot and Patricia was never affected in any way. All she knew was that her dad died through the war. I never ever mentioned it. It is only now, when she is 63, I get questions. How have I managed without a husband? Easy – by the time I was getting on my feet there was the odd fellow, but I was never interested enough to pursue. I'm now 88 years old. Don't regret a thing except the passing of Roy [her husband] who has missed his daughter, grandchildren and great-grandchildren. He is still with us and his picture is on the mantelpiece.

The 'picture on the mantelpiece' has much significance and is often mentioned. One boy always remembered the photographs displayed in the house next door where two widows, a mother and daughter, lived. One husband had been killed in the First World War and the other in the Second, a situation which was sadly not unusual. What is somewhat mystifying to the outsider is that so many widows revered the memory of the dead husband and did not – indeed, would not – remarry. Perhaps they felt it would be a betrayal. An article by Major Graham in the Kohima Educational Trust (KET) newsletter tells the story of Ellen Hannay. Lance Sergeant Robert Hannay of the Queen's Own Cameron Highlanders was killed in the crucial battle for Kohima in April 1944. The headstone in the Kohima war cemetery carries the inscription *Beatae Memoriae: Quis Nos Separabit?* (Blessed memories; Who will separate us?) Devastated by Robert's death, Ellen initially returned to live with her mother before getting a job overseas with the WVS, a job which took her to Calcutta; the closest she could get to her husband's resting place. Her first task was to arrange to visit his grave. It was to be the first of eight visits in her lifetime; her last pilgrimage was in 2000 and she died a

few days before her ninety-fourth birthday in April 2009. Hers is
a heart-rending tale of lifelong devotion to a memory. The story
of the KET itself is very affecting. It was set up in 2003 by the
few remaining survivors of the Kohima action in gratitude to the
local population of Nagaland for the unstinting support given to
the 2nd Division in those decisive two months in 1944. The KET
funds scholarships, libraries and tutoring for the Naga children
and an anonymous donor has funded a scholarship in Robert
Hannay's name, a fine memorial.

As discussed in an earlier chapter, many war widows had an
overwhelming need to see for themselves where their husbands were buried, or failing that, to have physical evidence (a
headstone for example) of that death. The question of government funding for these trips made regular appearances both in
Parliament and in the press in the 1980s. The young war widows
of today are at least spared that particular distress for not only are
their husbands' bodies brought home at government expense but
they are also given a military funeral. Some small comfort, but a
far cry from earlier times when one widow could not afford the
5s required for an inscription on her late husband's headstone.
They also know that their loss is a public one with wide coverage,
particularly on television; but are these widows thus less likely
to be 'sidelined'? The widows of three Australian pilots who
were killed when their aircraft crashed in 1993 asserted that the
military were insensitive and disorganised when communicating
with them. Once the men were buried they – the widows – were
out of sight and out of mind. Perhaps things do not change all
that much.

The KET was created in 2003 by the few remaining survivors of Kohima, and GLARAC (HM Ships *Glorious, Ardent* & *Acasta*
Association) was formed in 2002 principally by the children
of the men lost when the aircraft carrier HMS *Glorious* and
two attendant destroyers were sunk in the Norwegian fiasco
of June 1940 (during the withdrawl from Norway), an affair
somewhat skated over in the official histories. It is perhaps surprising that the offspring of those estimated 1,500 drowned

sailors are still so affected by that event some sixty-two years earlier. They determined to perpetuate the memory of those men and particularly to mark the seventieth anniversary year in 2010. A party travelled to Harstad in Norway, the last port of call in June 1940, where they were taken by a Norwegian tank landing craft to an area some 200 miles east of the position where the ships went down. There a family member from each of the three vessels laid a wreath, and a plaque was dedicated on shore. This was all followed by a memorial weekend at HMS *Drake*, Devonport, home port of the three ships, which included a dedication service with representatives from Norway and Malta (Malta because many Maltese had served on HMS *Glorious* when she was based with the Mediterranean Fleet). The significance of all this is that relatives, including a few widows, travelled amazing distances to pay their respects to the men lost at sea. Indeed 'not forgotten'.

Nowadays war widows have the WWA to speak for them; the current membership is in the thousands, but over the years these members have not been joined by substantial numbers of war widows. In 2009 there were approximately 4,500 WWA members of an estimated 34,000 women in receipt of a War Widow's Pension. A surprising number did not even know of its existence. The current website describes the association as essentially a pressure group which exists to improve the condition of war widows and their dependants in the United Kingdom. Its remit encompasses all those who have suffered bereavement as a result of the Second World War and all the conflicts which have involved British servicemen since then, lately those in Iraq and Afghanistan. The WWA also speaks on behalf of those affected by the loss of a husband post-war but whose death is attributable to his time in the service. It works with all government departments, petitioning for improvements in pensions, the administration of benefits and any other issues affecting their members. The association also represents war widows at national events, especially those of remembrance, and maintains close links with other relevant charitable organisations.

More recently the media have highlighted the difficulties experienced by families of deceased servicemen when the coroners conducting military inquests have little or no knowledge of military ethics or modern hostilities. Baroness Fookes DBE DL, current president of the WWA, led a campaign in the House of Lords to make it a requirement that any coroner conducting a military inquest should be thoroughly trained in the above before undertaking such an onerous duty. In the face of repeated government opposition she decided to call a Division (Parliamentary vote) and, supported by the Peers, obtained a handsome majority in favour of the motion. The government gracefully acquiesced and the requirement is now enshrined in the Coroners and Justice Act.

These days the WWA keeps in touch with its members via its newsletter *Courage* which updates them on the quirks and anomalies of the latest government legislation regarding the convoluted pensions system and anything else which may concern them. It also provides a forum for the opinions of and articles by the members. One young war widow who lost her husband in 2006 wrote a moving article on attending Remembrance weekend in 2008 and again in 2009. She found it an emotional experience, particularly the march along Whitehall on Remembrance Day itself:

> Remembrance Sunday was still overwhelming, especially when you see the numbers of veterans lined up for the march... There is a huge sense of respect for one another and cameraderie. The crowds are clapping and I'm still humbled, but have a much greater feeling of pride that all these people are showing support. One of our ladies commented that it is important to march, not only for my husband, but to represent those widows who regularly attended in the past and are now unable to do so.

She goes on to say that her own great aunt, a Second World War widow, used to march each year in memory of her husband and to honour all who had died in the service of their country. History, unfortunately, does repeat itself. When HRH the Prince of Wales, patron of the association, invited war widows to Highgrove, one member who was present with her own daughter wrote:

> I felt so sad when we spoke to the lovely young war widows, one had brought her small son of just a few months with her. Then seeing all the young widows looking so pretty in their summer dresses, talking and laughing, I turned to my daughter and said 'They are all so young, isn't it sad?' My dear daughter looked at me and said 'But Mum, you were young when you were widowed'. Do you know I had forgotten that I was young when I was widowed.

The WWA may well be part of the establishment now but it was mavericks like Jill Gee, Laura Connolly and Iris Strange who kick-started the process in 1971 and fought hard for every concession squeezed out of every reluctant government along the way.

The Falklands affair in 1982 probably marked the turning point in the nation's perception of war widows. The creation of the South Atlantic Fund gave material substance to pious sentiment. The few widows resulting from that conflict did not find themselves side-lined and ignored. The widow of Colonel H. Jones VC was invited to speak, take part in party politics and was present on the plat-form at a Conservative Party Conference. Christina Schmid, widow of Staff Sergeant Olav Schmid, killed in October 2009 trying to disarm an explosive device in Afghanistan, has taken a prominent role in speaking out on military pensions and other issues con-cerning the armed forces. She has presented a BBC 'Panorama' investigation into the work of bomb disposal officers and is a patron of Tickets for Troops, a charity set up to give servicemen free entry to sporting and music events. The contrast could not be more marked. Nothing can compensate the young widow for the premature loss of her husband but nowadays there is a great deal more financial and emotional support. For the women widowed by the First and Second World Wars it was a different story.

> There were no hand-outs like there is today, some people don't really know what hardship is, I'm afraid me and my Mum did.

My mother feels that people have no idea of the financial hardship and lack of support for Second World War widows.

My late mother raised five children on an income of about 30/- per week.

My Mum and other war widows she spoke to thought that they were more or less forgotten which made them bitter.

In reply to the question 'Do you think you have been treated fairly by successive governments?' one widow's answer was 'NO, NO, NO!' A fitting conclusion?

CURRENCY CONVERSION TABLE

1d (one penny)	approx. 0.4 new pence
6d (sixpence)	2½ new pence
1s (one shilling)	5 new pence
2s 6d (half a crown)	12½ new pence
10s (ten shillings)	50 new pence
20s (one pound)	100 new pence
1 guinea (£1 1s)	£1.05

SELECT BIBLIOGRAPHY

Boydell, Kate, *Death and how to Survive it* (Vermilion, 2005)

Goodall, Felicity, *Voices from the Home Front* (David & Charles, 2004)

Garfield, Simon, *We Are at War* (Ebury Press, 2005)

——, *Hidden Lives* (Ebury Press, 2005)

——, *Private Battles* (Random House, 2006)

Hanson, Neil, *Unknown Soldier* (Doubleday, 2005)

Harding, Brian, *Keeping the Faith: The History of the Royal British Legion* (Leo Cooper, 2001)

Kynaston, David, *Austerity Britain 1945–51* (Bloomsbury, 2007)

Marwick, Arthur, *British Society Since 1945* (Penguin, 2003)

Nicholson, Mavis, *What Did You Do in the War Mummy?* (Pimlico, 1995)

Nicholson, Virginia, *Singled Out* (Penguin, 2008)

Rathbone, Eleanor, *The Disinherited Family* (Falling Wall Press, 1986)

Raphael, Beverly, *The Anatomy of Bereavement, Handbook for the Caring Professions* (Routledge, 1990)

Sheridan, Dorothy, *Wartime Women* (Mandarin, 1990)

Smith, Lyn, *Young Voices* (Penguin, 2008)

Stevenson, John, & Chris Cook, *The Slump; Society and Politics During the Depression* (Quartet Books, 1979)

Summers, Julie, *Stranger in the House* (Simon & Schuster, 2008)

Turner, Barry, & Tony Rennell, *When Daddy Came Home* (Hutchinson, 1995)

Thorpe Clark, Mavis, *No Mean Destiny: The Story of the War Widows Guild* of *Australia 1945–1988* (Hyland House, 1986)

Waller, Maureen, *London 1945* (John Murray, 2005)

Articles

Lomas, Janis, 'War Widows in British Society' (Unpublished PhD thesis)

——, 'Delicate duties: issues of class and respectability in government policy towards the wives and widows of British soldiers in the era of the great war', *Women's History Review*, vol. 9, pp.123–147

——, '"So I Married Again": Letters from British Widows in the First and Second World Wars', *History Workshop Journal*, no. 38, pp.218–27

INDEX